A DAD
A BOY
AND
A BALL

A DAD
A BOY
AND
A BALL

George D. Durrant

Bookcraft

Salt Lake City, Utah

Library of Congress Catalog Card Number: 88-72240

ISBN 0-88494-678-9

First Printing, 1988

Printed in the United States of America

Contents

Introduction:
The Right Equipment

I don't know if there will be sports in heaven, but I do know there is a bit of heaven in sports. On the pages that follow are recorded some of the heavenly blessings our family has received because of what happened to us before, during, and after ball games.

The title of this book could have been *A Dad, a Family, and a Ball,* because sports experiences are of the most value when they involve the whole family. But because of a special focus on my son, Devin, I have chosen the title *A Dad, a Boy, and a Ball.* I chose Devin not because he is any more special than our other children, but rather because the experiences that life has brought him fit in so well with the direction this book has taken.

I've kept a journal for the past sixteen years. I began doing so in 1972 when Devin was eleven years old. On those personally sacred pages I've recorded much of what has happened in and to our family.

I have learned over the years that if you want to play basketball it's very useful to first have in your possession something resembling a basketball and a hoop. In other words, you need the right equipment to have a successful experience at any given sport. When I decided to write this book, I realized that if I wanted to accomplish something good with it I needed the right equipment. My journal provided the obvious court for my endeavor, while Devin's experiences offered the boundaries and the guidelines for becoming a true champion.

I use personal and family stories to support my point of view. In addition, I have extracted all the entries in my journal that relate to the relationship between Devin's sports career and me. These journal entries are interspersed throughout the book and they also comprise chapter 9. These experiences are not intended to do anything more than to show the blessings that have come to us through our interest and involvement in sports and other team-related activities—like family home evening. They provide the right equipment for this book. It is my hope in writing this book that it will help your family receive as many blessings as we have received, and even more.

The Pregame Show

Recently I said, "Son, you'd better get going or you'll be late for school. By the way, if you are going to miss one today, be sure it's a biology question and not a jump shot." When I made the above comment to my seventeen-year-old son, Mark, I was half kidding.

I'm not one of those fanatics who thinks that sports is everything. I will have to admit that I am fond of golf balls, tennis balls, pingpong balls, soccer balls, footballs, base-balls, softballs, and, most of all, basketballs. I like throwing balls, kicking balls, hitting balls, catching balls, and I really like shooting balls at baskets. If you were to tell me, "George, you have to go back now and live your life over without sports," I'd probably forfeit life. If I knew I had to live out my years without a single ball game to play in, or to see one of my kids play in, or to watch with Marilyn and the children, or to talk about with my family, or to discuss in the beginning of priesthood quorum meeting, I'd prob-ably just sit on the bench and stay in my pre-earth life.

About the only real disagreement I had with a friend of mine, who knows a lot about Church doctrine, was the time he said that there weren't going to be any ball games in heaven.

I started taking my young sons to athletic events before they could tell the players from the cheerleaders. Although basketball is my favorite game, I think going to a football game is among life's most glorious outings. A family can go to a football game and sit there in the brisk fall air, hear the band, sing the national anthem, and watch the kickoff. Such an activity creates in me a happiness beyond measure. Just writing about it makes me wish it were Saturday afternoon. I can see and feel it now. There is a nip in the air, and the leaves are red and yellow—we are just entering Cougar Stadium. It's such thoughts as these that make me think that God approves of ball games. I know that individuals like ball games, but I think that when athletics mix with family, sports can become one of life's genuine highlights.

Many years ago Marilyn, my young sons Matt and Devin, and I went to a BYU football game. The sky was overcast; the air was cold. It was a wonderful game because BYU (unusual in those days) was winning. Just as the second half began, a very wet half rain and half snow blew in. We were wearing warm coats, but we didn't have any kind of plastic protection or anything like that. As the weather worsened, my greatest fear was that Devin would get wet and cold, lose all interest in the game, and begin a campaign to go home. I couldn't bear that. It had been so long since BYU had beaten the University of Utah that I had to be there until the end even if we all froze to death. To ensure that we would not have to leave, I sat on the north side of our family where I could take most of the moisture that was pounding in on us. I held Devin next to me, trying to shield him from the wet, cold snow. But even though I pulled my big overcoat up over his head and had him snuggled close to me, it was futile. I just couldn't completely protect him. To keep his mind off from the cold I talked constantly to him:

"Now, watch that man! He's going to throw the ball. See it fly through the snow. The other man will catch it and then run. Watch . . . see him run. Oh, they got him!" Devin liked that kind of running narrative, but he was getting wet and cold. I'd wipe the water off his head with my handkerchief. Then I'd twist the soaked cloth to wring out the water. To my pleasant surprise, Devin didn't complain or ask to leave. Finally the storm was over. The sun came out. BYU was well ahead and victory was assured. I felt Devin move away from me and sit up straight in his own seat. Suddenly, he stood up and moved right in front of my knees. Facing me, he looked up and said, "Dad, you've done so much for me, isn't there something I can do for you?"

I had a hard time holding back the tears as I looked into his eyes. I replied, "Yeah, there is something you can do for me, Devin. You just be my son, just be my son." I sensed that he knew that I wanted him to go out in life and do good things. That moment with my family at a football game was a moment I will remember forever.

Oh, the joy of having a son or daughter who lives a life that makes you proud! They don't have to be stars in school or in sports, they just have to be stars in the game of life. If they do play sports, they don't have to be the star. They just have to do things to the best of their ability in whatever good things they choose to do.

But this book is about sports. So let's stick to the subject. We all know that the outcome of any sports event really doesn't matter. Yet participating in, or watching, or talking about who wins and who loses is a good way for a father and son and a family to work together to achieve victories that really do matter.

When we are young, we dream that we'll get the opening tip, score the first basket, keep the lead, win the game, and be a star. As our personal game of life wears on, that dream fades, and we dream a new dream—a dream that our children who are getting "near tipoff time" will become stars.

Thus it is that a young man's sweetheart becomes his spouse. The two of them rent a little house. A baby is born, and among the first toys is probably a doll and surely a ball. In the parents' hearts (at least in Dad's), will be a wish that the child will be fast and strong and tall.

Shortly after Marilyn and I were married, we were visiting in my home town of American Fork. The Cavemen's high school football team was great that year. The young star on the team was named Scholes. He had scored four touchdowns in the previous week's game. We were talking to his father, and he asked Marilyn what her maiden name was. She replied, "Burnham."

He excitedly exclaimed, "Burnham! The Scholes and the Burnhams are related." Boy, did that news excite me! In my mind I thought, "With those kind of genes coming from Marilyn's family and the great genes of the Durrants, we are likely to have children who are super athletes." That visionary thought was sort of like the opening tip, and I could hardly wait for the future game to begin.

I sensed then, and I know even more now, that seeing one of my children play ball is a greater thrill than playing it myself.

Yes, we sports dads do often dream that our boys will grow up to be athletes. All of my sons and one of my daughters turned out that way to some degree. Some of them were better than others, but that's the way it is with nearly everything. Besides, dreaming about things has always been one of the main ingredients of happiness. If the dreams come true, that's just an added bonus.

I went to almost all the games in which my children played. Whether they starred or sat on the bench, my wholesome pride was equal. Oh, sometimes my outward pride was greater when my son was a star. When that happens parents receive a little more recognition, but that's pretty shallow. A player doesn't have to be a star to make a move that he's never made before or try like he's never tried before. The quiet inward pride of seeing a son do a little better than ever before is the kind of pride that can make an everlasting difference in determining life's champions. Of course musical instruments, dancing shoes, and drama stages can do for a family the same thing as sports. But I'll have to let experts on those things write those stories.

About the prettiest picture I can create in my mind is the scene of a dad and a boy and a ball. It seems to me that a ball can tie a father and son together like little else can. A ball can close a difficult gap between a dad and a boy. It can also help a mom and a whole family dream together, talk together, and live together in love and closeness.

And lest you think I'm leaving out girls, some of my greatest athletic thrills came as I watched my daughter, Sarah, play. I recall that one night before her most important game, she called me to her room and said, "Father, I need a blessing." Her voice choked with emotion as she added, "I've just got to play well tomorrow night. We've got to beat Olympus."

In an attempt to comfort her, I said, "Come on, Sarah. Don't take it so seriously. It's just a game."

"No, Father. It's not just a game, because their center has been calling my boyfriend, and if they win I just know I'll lose him." I could see this was indeed more than a game and so I prayed with all my might.

The next day I cheered myself hoarse. We lost—and she lost him, too. Now, looking back and realizing how young she was, I'm not sure we really lost at all. On second thought, I believe we were the winners.

Family life just seems to be more well oiled when there is a ball game coming up out on the front lawn, or at the cultural hall, or at the high school gym, or at the twenty-three-thousand-seat Marriott Center. Before the game, there is the surprise of what might happen. During the game, there is the excitement of what is happening. And after the game, there is the expert analysis of what did happen. The profound lessons that come from experiencing the joy of victory and the agony of defeat arc not felt anywhere nearly as keenly as they are within the sacred walls of home.

That concludes our pregame show. My prediction is that families who love sports will be the big winners in the wonderful game of life.

Journal: August 1972–April 1975

August 25, 1972. Our Kentucky home became complete today because in the evening two of our office Elders helped the boys and me put up a basketball standard at the south end of the parking lot. [We had just moved to Louisville, Kentucky, to begin our three-year mission.]

March 24, 1973. Devin got a trophy today for being chosen one of the league all-stars. In the evening, as he was going to his bedroom he said, "Pops, come and see me before I go to sleep."

I replied, "I'm too tired."

"Pops, if you knew how much it means to me to talk to you, you'd come."

With such an invitation I followed him to his bedroom. He spoke, "Pops, talk to me."

"What should I say?" I asked.

"Tell me what you think of my trophy. Did you ever make an all-star team, Pops?"

That got us going and we talked of many things—things that mattered much more than trophies. Finally Devin said, "Pops, thanks for coming. Sure love you, Pops."

I arose, bent down, and kissed him on the forehead and said, "I love you too. Goodnight."

January 28, 1974. Devin had a basketball game tonight. He's in the eighth grade, but he plays on the ninth-grade team. He made 31 points—he's good. Coach Bolis has really been hard on him but it has paid off. Once Devin told him, "Let me play on the eighth-grade team. That's where I belong." The coach said, "You go right ahead. But if you do I'm through working with you." Devin stuck it out on the ninth-grade team.

June 21, 1974. Devin won a trophy for winning a one-on-one contest at a basketball camp that he and Matt attended in North Carolina.

January 11, 1975. Attended Devin's basketball game in the morning. He had a bad back, but he did well. He's good.

February 1, 1975. Spent the morning at Devin's game. He won but he appeared a little slow. He looks pale. I feel he needs a good physical.

February 8, 1975. Saw Devin play this morning. He made 23 points and really played well. He is a good player.

February 15, 1975. Attended Devin's game at eleven-thirty. He carried his team. He scored all the team's points in the first overtime. He made a foul pitch with one second to go in the second overtime to win the game. As he prepared to shoot I prayed. I suppose the Lord doesn't care if a game is won or lost, but I couldn't help but pray.

February 28, 1975. Devin played a great game tonight. He sure has a future. He scored 23 points.

March 1, 1975. Went to Devin's ball game in the morning. His team won the Jefferson County Junior High School Championship. After the game the coach's mother told us that her son knows that we are going to move back to Utah this summer. He'd like Devin to stay and live with him. She said her son had said, "Devin is not just an exciting ball player but a fine young man and the only student to whom I ever gave an A + ."

April 3, 1975. Attended Matt and Devin's basketball banquet. Coaches announced to the group that they were sorry Matt was graduating and that they are praying Devin won't leave Kentucky.

2

The Home Court Advantage

Playing the game of life well on your home court guarantees that you'll play it well wherever you go. That's not always true in sports. When I was a boy, my home court was in the barn. In those days, the Cavemen from American Fork High School were known for losing the big ones. We'd been in the state basketball finals more than any other team. But we'd lost every time. The newspapers just kept in reserve the headline, "American Fork—A Bridesmaid But Never a Bride." As a boy I didn't know what a bridesmaid was but I sure knew the sorrow that came from losing.

I was determined to change things and to win a crown for the Cavemen. That's why I practiced hours on end. When the weather was good, I'd play outside. The cow also spent a lot of time on our dirt court. She didn't play ball there, but what she did do sort of affected my game. That is why I was good at shooting, but I wasn't much on dribbling. When the snows came, I had to move into the barn. The further we got into winter, the more hay my father fed to our jersey cow. As the hay stack in the barn got smaller, my playing space grew. In December and January I didn't have room to shoot much more than a lay-up. But by March, with three-fourths of the hay gone, I had room to practice my long jumper.

My older brothers had helped me build the basket inside the barn. We made it by cutting off the top rim of one of the round wooden containers that the clabbered milk came in. We purchased the sour white stuff from the poultry plant to feed the chickens so they'd lay milk-white eggs. To help our homemade hoop withstand the constant bombardment of basketballs, we took an old bicycle tire and tied it around the wooden rim with twine. The circumference of the tire-covered wooden rim was not much bigger than the basketball itself. As a matter of fact, it might have even been a little bit smaller. With the necessity of hitting that kind of target, it was no wonder that I became a deadly shooter.

I'd go out to the barn on a cold March day, pick up the ball, stand way back in the distant corner, and shoot right up over the rafter. I knew just how to gauge the shot so that it would hit nothing but where the net should have been. Up over the rafter the ball would sail. Down it would drop right in the middle of that basket. It would vibrate violently a quarter of an inch each way, then fall down on to the barn floor. I'd glance around, hoping somebody was looking in the barn window, but they never were. Each day, out on my home court, I'd shoot long shot after long shot. Incredibly, almost each one found the mark. The only thing that could stop me was to have somebody else come in. Then things wouldn't work with the great precision I'd formerly employed.

As our children grew up, I told them many bedtime stories about my home court and how I'd hit long shot after long shot. Hearing this they would get all excited and say, "Daddy, we want to have a gym like you had when you were a boy." But unfortunately for my children, we never had enough money for a barn or a pig pen or a coal house or a cellar or a whole lot of important things like that.

As we raised our family, I changed jobs quite often. Because of that our family moved a lot. Each time we considered purchasing a new home, a prime consideration was always whether there was a suitable place on the property to build a basketball court. That was a more important matter than whether the house had indoor plumbing.

As we would walk around the prospective property, I'd say to the boys, "Look! Right there is a perfect spot for our basketball court." They would excitedly agree and the realtor would know he had a deal.

After we got moved in, we'd all go out and clear off the land. We'd put some nice straight two-by-four planks around the outside borders. We'd get everything level and estimate the number of square yards of concrete we'd need. Then I'd call my old friends Wayne Lynn and Lee Miller. They'd get there just as the cement truck would. Words just won't allow me to describe the excitement my boys and I would feel as we'd see that cement get smoother and smoother. Wayne knew how to finish it so it looked real good. The boys would all help as best they could. Even as I write this now, it makes me want to turn back time and build a home basketball court again with my sons.

The boys weren't often the hardest of workers, but when we were building a basketball court they worked themselves nearly to death. In a day or two the cement would be hard. We'd put up the pipes that my friend Bob Cutler had welded for us. Then we'd attach our homemade wooden backboard. Next the hoop would be bolted at the precise height. After that we'd play and play and play.

In the days that followed, I'd come home from work tired. The boys would ask me to come out and shoot a few. At first I'd say, "No, I'm too tired." They'd persist and I'd give in. Once out on the home court, I'd discover that I wasn't really tired at all. Oh, I was tired of office work and things like that. But I wasn't tired of important things like basketballs and boys. Out there, new energy would flow into my body and I'd really come to life.

Sometimes when I was just too tired to play ball with the kids or when I had to go away, I'd tell them to go out and play on their own. To motivate them to do so, I'd tell them about my friend Purnham Purnham.

My story went like this. As a young boy, my older brothers would go with their friends and I was often left to play alone. That didn't stop me from having a real competitive match. I'd just use my imagination to conjure up an invisible friend whom I named Purnham Purnham.

I'd grab the old worn ball and shout, "Come on, Purnham Purnham. Let's go in the barn and have a little game of basketball." Other people told my mom that her son George talked to himself. But I wasn't talking to myself. I was talking to Purnham Purnham. Purnham Purnham was always willing to play, and in a few minutes the game would begin.

I'd shoot the ball the first time for me and then I'd shoot the second time for Purnham Purnham. I'd keep the score. If Purnham Purnham got close to winning, I'd deliberately miss a few shots for him. But if unluckily those shots accidently went in and I sensed that he was about to win. I'd just dissolve him out of my mind and he'd be gone. I never once lost to Purnham Purnham. My children listened intently. Finally I would say, "Purnham Purnham was a great shooter and could dribble and pass like a pro, but I always thrashed him." The children seemed impressed. Well, sort of, anyway.

But when time allowed, and that was real often, playing against those young sons was pure joy. It was especially fun when they were little. In those wonderful days I used to win. Then, for a while, I was able to gain a few more victories because I doubled as both a player and as the referee. As time went by, they gradually learned the rules and began to protest many of my calls. That forced me to give up the refereeing aspect of the game. After that I lost every time. That's when I started trying for the sportsmanship trophy. But even that was hard to win because of feelings I'd get when my boys ridiculed me. I'd throw up a hook shot that never used to fail me back in the barn. Now it would be an air ball. I'd stumble when they faked right and went left. They'd score and then they'd laugh at me and say, "Pops, I'll bet you never were as good as you said you were." Those comments would get me pretty upset, and I could feel the sportsmanship trophy slipping away.

Not long ago I played against Mark, my youngest. When I could see that defeat was inevitable and that he was acting pretty smug, I called time out. I looked up into his eyes and said, "Mark, let me tell you something. Let's put my athletic prowess into the proper perspective. You and I know that there will be a resurrection."

Mark is a religous young man, so he was interested. I continued, "When the resurrection occurs, our bodies will come back to life. Once again the strength we had when we were at our prime will return. When that happens and my full physical powers return, I'll meet you again on the court. I'll go one-on-one with you, just as we are doing today. Then, I assure you, my young son, my hook shot will hit dead center and I'll block every shot you put up. Then it will be me who will hit long shot after long shot. It will be me who will fake right and go left. It will be me who will soar high for each rebound. The results will then be much different than they are now." I detected that Mark was trembling a bit, so I threw him the ball and we resumed the game.

The greatest victory I ever won was on our home court. My oldest son, Matt, was in the ninth grade. He wanted with all his heart to be an athlete. He was pretty good at basketball, but he wasn't growing much. During that period of time he was pretty ornery. He would seldom talk to me, and when he did it was in an unpleasant tone. Yet I'd heard that over at school he was the most friendly and amiable boy on campus.

I wanted him to talk to me because I felt that something was troubling him. My desires for such a conversation had not yet been rewarded. One day we were out playing basketball before dinner, just the two of us. We were playing a good game of one-on-one. I'd score and then he'd score. While we were playing, I started talking to him. I asked him, "How did it go in school today?" His only answer was an uncomfortable silence. I raised my voice and asked, "Did you hear me? How did it go at school today?"

Finally he answered, "Why do you ask such dumb questions?"

A bit surprised at his abrupt reply, I thought to myself, "I guess that was a dumb question." I decided to upgrade my queries. I asked, "What did you have for school lunch?"

He replied, "What does that matter? Every day we have the same dumb stuff."

I wasn't quite sure just what to ask him next. We shot a few more baskets. In my silence I was wishing he wasn't so unhappy. Then an inspired question came to me. I asked, "How did it go in gym today?"

His countenance brightened as he enthusiastically replied, "Hey, in gym today I did pretty good, Father." He started talking to me. We bounced the ball a little less and just stood around between baskets. As our conversation thickened, he spoke with some emotion.

"Dad, I don't know if you ever wonder why I'm so ornery."

I replied, "Oh, no. I never wonder about that," and he continued.

"Well, the reason is that I don't like the way I look." I was silent for a few seconds. Then I spoke.

"You look good. You look just like me." With that he kind of gulped with a slight indication of pain.

"No, Dad, you look all right but I don't. I'm not as big as I want to be and I wear glasses. When I look at myself in the mirror, I just don't look like an athlete."

I knew what he was talking about. As a youth, I'd had some of those same problems. He kept talking to me, and I didn't know what to say. I could have said, "Don't be silly. You look like an athlete. You'll grow one of these days so don't worry about it. You'll be a great athlete." But I didn't give those pat answers. I just listened and I thought and I cared.

Just then Marilyn called and told us to come to dinner. We left the basketball court and walked across the back lawn. As we passed under the big trees I put my arm around his shoulder. We climbed up the back stairs. There was a feeling of love and understanding between us. I hadn't answered any of his questions, but he'd had a chance to tell me, his dad, how he felt and that had helped him.

That big-time victory took place because during those meaningful moments there was just a dad, a boy, and a ball together on our home court. That one sacred experience was worth ten times more than the cost of a thousand yards of concrete. It seems like the only time my children ever talk to me is when I'm with them. Sports, especially on the home court, gives me many opportunities to be with them. And it's hard to lose when you have the home court advantage.

Journal: September 1975 – March 1976

September 27, 1975. We've built a basketball court out back. [We were now back in Utah, and it was the beginning of Devin's sophomore year at Provo High School.] We poured the cement ourselves about three Saturdays ago. Six of our returned missionaries helped us. It cost us $225 for cement. The kids, especially Devin, love to play there.

Devin, who will be a sophomore when school starts, is now 6'3". He appears to be on his way to being an excellent basketball player. Coach Spencer raves about his ability to pass the ball.

November 10, 1975. Devin was put on the varsity today. He needs $25 shoes and $6 for a uniform. Money is tight, but somehow we'll get him what he needs.

November 20, 1975. Tonight attended a basketball meeting with Devin's coach. He said "Devin is great. I've only had one other player who had the total court awareness that he has."

January 9, 1976. Went to Devin's game. He made 10 points in the first of his J.V. game. Then the sophomore coach came in at half-time and said, "We are losing. We need Devin." He then went to the other gym and made 22 points in the second half of the sophomore game. He is about 6'4" when measured in the morning. [I always tried to keep track of his height. But I could never really get it correct.]

January 23, 1976. Went to Devin's ball game tonight. Dwight rode with me. Devin scored 22 points in J.V. game but didn't play in varsity.

February 6, 1976. Attended Devin's J.V. game today. He scored 36 points. His two free throws with ten seconds left won the game.

March 3, 1976. Devin made 30 points in a losing cause against the Orem sophomores. The game went into two overtimes. He's a pressure player. I'm so proud of him I can't describe it. What a fine young man! He is such a good friend of mine. He got in a varsity game also and played with composure. The fans seem to like him.

March 9, 1976. Devin gets bigger each week. He sure plays smooth.

March 11, 1976. Devin says he feels he will be one of, if not the first, sub in the state tournament games. That makes me nervous.

March 16, 1976. Attended state tournament tonight. Provo beat Cottonwood 77 to 55. Devin played the last two minutes. We had the game won when he came in, but I sure was nervous and proud.

March 18, 1976. Attended basketball tournament in Salt Lake City. Provo beat West by 6. It was a great game.

March 19, 1976. Went to the basketball tournament in Salt Lake with Matt. During the pregame warmup we had a great talk. I told him how much it meant to me to have him set such a pattern for the rest of our children to follow. I told him that Devin idolized him. Matt replied, "I doubt if any brother ever loved a brother like I love that kid down there warming up on the floor." I nearly cried as we sat there in the bleachers and talked about our family and Matt's future mission to Japan. Provo lost the game by 3. They had a chance but couldn't do it. Skyline had a player named Vranes who scored 38 points. He was great.

3

The Starting Lineup

In the game of life there is something satisfying about being a starter instead of a sub. But even being a sub in sports can often help us win a starting nod in life. When my oldest son, Matt, gained a regular position on the Seneca High School team, I told him that I understood. I proudly announced, "I was a three-year starter for my ward team, and one year was chosen all-stake. But," I said as I spoke to all my children, "You don't have to be a starter to be a star. During my senior year in high school, my dream of being a starter for the American Fork Cavemen had long since eroded away. It seemed that the coach liked me best. So during the games he had me sit on the bench near him. In my heart I always felt that the time would come when I'd be needed in the game. Finally destiny beckoned and I was ready."

By now the children were listening with great interest. I continued, "One Friday night American Fork was playing Brigham Young High School. It was a crucial game—perhaps the most important game in all recorded history. Our main center, LeRoy Griffin, was called for three fouls in the first half. His fourth came at the beginning of the second half. I'm sure the coach considered taking Griff out to save him for the final minutes. Then he looked down the bench at me and decided the only hope was to keep old Griff in there. Three minutes later he was whistled for his fifth foul. Now came one of those long time outs designed to allow the coach time to figure out what to do. Again he looked down the bench at me. He looked away, then in apparent anguish he looked back at me again and said. 'George, get your sweat suit off.' I did. My time had come.

"The game was tied. American Fork was playing well. Up until this terrible moment it looked as if we at least had a remote possibility of beating this top-rated group of superstars. But now without Griff it appeared that all was lost.

"My cousin Boyd Durrant was a policeman. He could go anywhere in the gym that he wanted. He came down, touched me on the shoulder, and said, 'George, don't go out there and embarrass our family. You get out there and you play.'

"Knowing that I was needed, I played better than I had ever played. I jumped high and I gathered in rebounds. I did all that I needed to do. The game went back and forth, back and forth. In the last quarter the lead must have changed hands five or six times. Finally we were down to the last minute. The game was tied. I hadn't scored any points, but I had defended and rebounded and passed without error. With thirty seconds to go I was fouled. There wasn't any one-and-one rule back then—I just had one shot. With the score tied and thirty seconds to go, I stood up to the line. Usually I had stage fright when I was playing, but I didn't now. I had to make it. The fate of all mankind was in my hands. The referee gave me the ball: I took a deep breath, and shot it. It was in! Now if we could just hold on.

"We came down the floor, and Harold Christenson, the best to ever play for B.Y. High, got the ball and scored. We were down by one with only ten seconds to go. We brought the ball across midcourt. Max Smith passed it to old Spud Stiener. Spud was left-handed and wasn't known for his great accuracy as a long-range shooter, or even a short one for that matter. But time was about to run out so he had to fire it up.

"The shot was kind of at an angle out on the side. I was right under the basket, and I watched the ball fly towards its target. It was off course just a little. That caused it to kiss the backboard enough to put it on course. It swished through the net and dropped sweetly into my hands. The game was over. I'll always remember the coach coming out and taking me into his arms. Together we cried tears of joy. I had only made one point that night, but we won the game by that one point. I was needed. I was a sub but I was needed."

After I had finished that exciting story we were having some refreshments. Marilyn handed me the largest piece of banana cream pie. I could tell she knew she was serving a superstar. As I ate I could see all the children looking at me just like I'd seen kids look at Larry Bird. I had my pen ready, but strangely enough none of them asked me for my autograph.

My son Warren was a large ninth-grader when we moved from Provo to Salt Lake City. Coaches in his new school were sure he'd be able to play because his brother Devin was a BYU star. Warren tried, but his gentle and re-markable talents weren't those of a smoothly coordinated athlete.

Warren really didn't have the intense interest or the de-sire needed to improve his game. He wanted to give up high school athletics and pursue other matters. At the time, I couldn't understand that. I pressured him to at least try.

He did for a while, but he finally said, "I don't want to play any more." His mother supported him and empha-sized, "It's his decision." This hurt me greatly, but I learned to live with it.

After that he played for the church team. I became his coach. My whole tactic of coaching was to sit on the bench and shout, "Way to go, Warren!" "Good shot, Warren!" "Way to jump, Warren!" He'd look over at me on the sideline and smile. Warren was playing basketball the way it ought to be played on all levels. He was just plain having fun. He was doing his best, and I, his father, was praising his every move. After each game, I'd put my arm around him and say, "That was a great game, Warren." We—a dad, a boy, and a ball—established a relationship that I don't think we could have developed in any other way.

Maybe my friend was right. Maybe there won't be sports in heaven. I know this, however; our family sure has found a lot of heaven in sports. I know there will be a starting lineup of sorts up there. Ball games will have done much to help each of our family want to be starters for the heavenly hosts.

Journal: August 1976–March 1977

August 4, 1976. [Devin was attending a BYU basketball camp just prior to his high school junior year.] Saw Devin play tonight. He seemed lackadaisical. I criticized him severely. He took it well.

August 6, 1976. Attended Devin's all-star game at the BYU basketball camp. He did well playing with the best of them. He is a good one. But at 6'5", he looked small among the 6'10" guys. He played a game in the evening. He did very well, but his team lost.

October 14, 1976. Devin just started his junior year and he is about 6'5" now.

November 26, 1976. Devin played a great game as his team beat Highland by 20 points. He is so confident and sure. I feel that he has a brilliant future. But of course his mission will supercede his career.

December 7, 1976. Devin made 9 points, 15 rebounds, 5 assists, and 3 steals against Viewmont.

December 14, 1976. Devin played tonight. They defeated Layton by about 30. He made 13.

December 29, 1976. Devin Played magnificently and with 17 points was high-point man. Provo won their tenth straight with no trouble.

January 14, 1977. Went to game at Hillcrest. Neither team had lost all season but Provo really beat them badly. Devin had 14 points in first quarter and 19 by half. He only got 2 in second half, but by then game was really over.

February 4, 1977. Went to Devin's game against Orem in the Marriott Center. A big crowd was on hand. Devin was tight for 3 quarters. The last quarter he was a star. Ended with 12 points. Including two game-winning free throws in overtime. He shot them after a time out. All eyes were on him. He made one and then the other. BYU Coach Harry Anderson was impressed with him and said, "We must invite him to some BYU games. He is a super ballhandler." I told Devin. He was thrilled to have BYU interested in him.

February 25, 1977. Devin made 27 points tonight and slam-dunked one. He looked great. Game was at Kearns. Provo 83, Kearns 50.

March 8, 1977. I talked to a Weber State assistant coach tonight at the game. They are interested in Devin. They feel he will be a great one. He had 19 points tonight. Provo 80, Granger 49.

March 14, 1977. State tournament started today. Provo played at 4:30, and defeated East High 89 to 52. Devin had a cold first half. He warmed up in the second half and got 12 points. He looked real good. He is smooth. It's thrilling to have a son such as he is.

March 17, 1977. I worry in every spare minute about Devin's game tomorrow. It is billed as the "Game"; I'll be glad when it is over. Devin is in good shape. He will do well in the big game.

March 18, 1977. A sad day. Provo 44, Skyline 46.

A last-second shot by Skyline's star center, Danny Vranes, did Provo in. Devin only had five points. At home tonight we had a special evening with Devin. Kath massaged his shoulders, and Marilyn and I talked to him. He received several phone calls of congratulation. We heard that Coach Pimm of the U of U said on the radio that he is interested in Devin. That was quite a thrill. He supposedly said, "There are two players who really look good. One is Devin Durrant. We want him."

4

Watching Our Heroes

Life seems to have more direction when we have some heroes to watch, to admire, and to emulate. One of my family's first sports heroes was Rich Haws.

When Matt and Devin became old enough to understand about a state high school basketball tournament, we got in the car and with unbounded excitement headed up to watch the semi-finals. I can still remember walking into the Special Events Center on the University of Utah campus. We got ourselves a hot dog with a lot of mustard on it and climbed up to our high-level seats.

Weber High School was playing somebody. As we watched, I became aware that one player was different from the rest. His name was Haws. He was a superb athlete. But that wasn't what made him different. It was his demeanor, the way he smiled and acted. I wish I could describe it better, but it was just that "something" you see only once in a while. I was hoping my boys would catch a vision of what a real athlete could be.

"Matt and Devin," I said excitedly, "Watch number seven. See how he acts. See how hard he plays. See how he treats the referee."

A technical foul was called on the other team. Haws strode up the foul line to shoot the desperately needed point. The coach called him back; he wanted one of the little guards to shoot it. Haws looked at the coach for a minute like, "Come on, Coach. Let me shoot it." Then he smiled. As the players all lined up, Haws quickly ran to the other player who stood at the foul line. He reached over and ruffled the little guard's hair. The guard smiled, took the ball, and swished it through. Haws did something for the whole team.

I said to the boys, "That's the kind of player you want to be. You don't want to get on the referee's case, and you don't want to get down on yourself. Just get out there and have a good time."

On that special night Rich Haws became a hero to my boys. Through the years, I've reminded them about the night when we saw Haws play. Haws didn't know what he did for my family, but I'm sure glad he did it.

I wanted my sons to have heroes so much that I even made one up—his name was Rip Snorgan. At bedtime I'd tell the children some Rip Snorgan stories. Here is a typical one.

Rip Snorgan was the greatest basketball player of all time. Once his team was behind by ten points and there were only thirty seconds left in the game. All the fans were leaving because they all knew that no team could win when they were behind by ten points with only half a minute to go. But Rip apparently didn't know because he went to work.

Rip's team had the ball and threw it to him. He quickly turned and shot. As he did so he made certain that he was fouled. He made the shot and went to the foul line to shoot the foul. He deliberately missed the foul shot, bounded in, got the ball, and shot again. He of course made the shot, and while shooting made sure that he was fouled. He again deliberately missed the foul shot, jumped in, got the ball, and shot again. Of course he made the shot and again was fouled. He continued to do this until there was only one second to go and the score was tied. Then he stepped to the line and sank the winning free throw. His team was victorious by just one point.

Then I'd say to the amazed children, "Now you may wonder how Rip Snorgan could perform such sports heroics. The answer is that his girlfriend was the cheerleader. Her name was Fanny Foofoo, and she was the best cheerleader of all time. Rip liked her a lot and always tried to make her proud of him. They were heroes to each other." The children seemed satisfied with that logical explanation. They seldom fell asleep during a Rip Snorgan story.

Of course, real heroes are much better than fictional ones. Devin never was a hero to our family. It's hard to have a hero who lives in your own house. On the other hand, he had a teammate by the name of Steve Trumbo — now there was a hero! To us he was a cross between Rip Snorgan and Jack Armstrong, the all-American boy. We loved it when Devin would tell us Steve Trumbo stories. Once Devin told us that as the BYU team flew home from El Paso, they got in to some terrible air turbulence. The plane was rocking every direction. Devin said, "I was scared. This frightening experience lasted several minutes. Danny Ainge was sitting next to Steve Trumbo on one side of the aisle, with Alan Taylor and me across from them. Danny leaned over to Alan and said, 'Alan, I think we're going down. I'll see you in the celestial kingdom.' Then he looked at me and said, 'Devin, I'll see you in the celestial kingdom.' He looked at Steve and, after a slight pause, said, 'Trumbo, it's been real nice knowing you.' "

Our family all agreed that if our hero, Steve Trumbo, wasn't going to be in heaven we weren't sure we wanted to be.

On another occasion Devin said, "Our most consistent Cougar of all time [let's call him Jim Snodgrass] had a foul shot at the end of a game that could have helped us beat New Mexico. But in a manner that was not like him, he missed it and we lost. That crucial loss put us all in a deep depression. As we were waiting in the airport to fly on to El Paso, no one was very talkative. It was late at night and we were all tired. We were all sitting around with our heads down because of the heartbreaking defeat. Unknown to any of us, Steve Trumbo made his way over to the ticket counter. Quietly he gave a message to the man there. A few seconds later, an announcement came over the public address system, saying: "Would Choke Snodgrass please report to the United Airlines counter . . . Choke Snodgrass please report to the United Airlines counter."

"Every one of us, including the coach, nearly fell out of our seats laughing. The spell had been broken. We were happy again." Hearing this story caused our family to rejoice at our hero's antics.

Another hero of ours was Rick Monday, who played outfield for the Los Angeles Dodgers. During the time of the Vietnam War protests, there was much dissension in the country, expressed by flag burning and other anti-American demonstrations. Just prior to the beginning of one Dodgers game, two men jumped out of the bleachers and onto center field. Then, in full view of thirty thousand fans, they started to burn an American flag. Rick Monday was not far away, awaiting the beginning of the game. When he first saw the two men, he was not fully aware of what was happening. Then he saw the flag and the small flame.

He took off on a dead run towards them. Being a large man, he didn't slow down—he ran right over both of them. They went sprawling to the ground. He gathered up the flag into his arms. As the silent but amazed fans looked on, he trotted all the way to the infield. The organist, seeing what was happening, caught the spirit and started playing "God Bless America." Rick Monday gently handed the flag to the umpire. The fans, who by this time were standing, broke into a tearful applause. As our family read that story, Rick Monday became our hero. We sat silently for several seconds. Then with a voice choked with emotion, I said softly, "I love this country and I love all of you." We all felt a deep sense of gratitude for all the freedoms and blessings that we have in this choice land.

Another hero who encouraged our family was a linebacker in the NFL. During a championship game a field goal kicker known for his exceptional consistency and accuracy missed one, then two, crucial three-point kicks. With just a few seconds to go his team was down by one point. They could have been winning if he had hit either of his first two attempts. Now with the ball on the opponent's thirty-yard line, he had a chance to redeem himself by kicking the winning field goal. The ball was snapped. It was placed down. He kicked it. It was just a foot or so wide to the left. This had been the most important game played that year, but because of his errant kick his team lost.

After the game the television cameras focused on the happy celebrations of the victors. Then a closeup camera shot appeared on the screen. It showed the anguished kicker sitting on the bench with his helmet off and head bowed down. All the other players had moved away, and he sat alone. Suddenly an all-star linebacker from the other team came toward him. As the camera focused on the scene, the massive opponent touched the kicker's shoulder. Then he spoke, but the sound of his words were not picked up by the microphone. The dejected kicker lifted his head and looked up into the eyes of his opponent. As the linebacker walked away, the kicker's eyes followed him. It was obvious that something had changed. The kicker's expression was that of inspiration and hope.

Later a sensitive television announcer asked the kicker, "What did he say to you?"

The kicker replied, "He just said three words: 'Christ still lives.' "

We talked about what our new hero had done and what it meant. We knew again that there is no lasting defeat in a world where we know that Christ still lives.

Another of our family's heroes was a giant basketball player. After Devin returned from a week of practicing in preparation for competition in the 1983 University Games, he told us this story:

"I roomed with a 6'11" guy. During our association together, we had opportunities to discuss religion. One afternoon, I was alone in my room kneeling in prayer. My roommate came in unexpectedly. When he saw me on my knees, he stopped and turned off the 'Walkman' music he was listening to. He stood there without moving until I finished my prayer. This experience led us both to think a little bit more about religion.

"A few days later, after our practice, most of the guys were on an elevator going up to our rooms. As we rode up, some of the other members of the team started using some foul language. I was standing next to my roommate at that time. When he heard this language, he suddenly said to all of those big all-American athletes, 'Hey, you guys! Don't talk that way around my friend here (pointing at me).' I looked back at all of them and said, 'You guys can talk anyway you want.' But that wasn't good enough for my friend. As the door opened up for us to go back to our rooms, he said to all of them, 'I hope you're not talking like that when The Man comes.' Some of them looked at him kind of perplexed, so he repeated his great speech, 'I hope you're not talking like that when The Man comes.'

"I was impressed that my big friend had the courage to tell these super athletes that they'd better get their lives shaped up and clean up their language in preparation for the day when the Savior will come back again to this earth."

Often when we speak of our heroes, we don't just talk about having heroes, we talk about the need to be a hero. Not just a sports hero, but a hero in the game of life. I told the kids: "Hey, it's a tough game out there in the world. Our opponent is a real competitor. He plays hard and smart and unfair. To win we'll have to play to the best of our ability and then some. But that is the way we like it. We don't like to play in a one-sided game. That doesn't produce heroes.

"We don't like it when the team we are about to play has lost twenty-six straight; we hardly feel like going out on the floor.

"The type of game we get up for is when we play a team that won it all last year—a team that has won nineteen in a row. Then things are different. On such a night we can feel the strength and energy surging through our bodies as we get our moral ankles taped and lace up our spiritual Adidas. We say to each other, 'Tonight we are going to play the toughest team we'll ever face. They feel they are going to win it all. But we know differently. Tonight we've got them on our home court. We've got the Great Coach on our side. Tonight we are going to win.'

"So, kids, let's practice on our home court and then go out into the world and be spiritual, moral, honorable warriors in the great game of life. Let's go out on the world's court and make a difference. Let's go out and be heroes."

Journal: July 1977–December 1977

July 1, 1977. Coaches Frank Arnold and Harry Anderson came to our house tonight. They spent two hours with us. They want Devin at the Y. They feel he is one of the twelve best prospects in America. They were most enthusiastic. I felt honored to have them in our home. I'm sure this is the first of many approaches that will come to Devin as the year goes on. He is 6'6" now and is really improving all the time. The coaches suggested that they didn't want Devin to go on a mission until he'd played out four years. So that is going to be a problem.

July 14, 1977. Saw Devin play basketball tonight. He is about the best I've seen in high school.

August 23, 1977. Coach Arnold told Devin his defense was atrocious.

August 30, 1977. He had a phone call from Idaho State's Coach. They want him. He practices each day at the Y.

September 1, 1977. Today Devin received letters from some ten colleges who are interested in him coming to play ball for them.

September 3, 1977. Went to BYU with Devin. He lifted weights. He has muscle. He weighs 187 pounds. He also shot foul pitches while I threw the ball back to him.

October 5, 1977. I came home at eight o'clock, and Coach Jerry Pimm of the U of U and his assistant came to our house. They spent two hours here. They showed us a movie of U of U basketball. They were really impressive. If BYU wasn't around, the U of U would be it. I was really impressed with Coach Pimm. It is fun to see Devin so sought after. I'm real proud of him.

November 10, 1977. Devin's back is hurting him.

November 16, 1977. Devin's back is still sore. He tried to practice today but he couldn't. He went for more treatment. He and I had a long talk about it. I'm sure that he is discouraged, but he keeps a cheerful attitude. I called the BYU trainer who is working with him. The trainer feels that a week's rest with treatments and swimming will help.

November 17, 1977. Went to see BYU intrasquad game. A fellow named Ainge looked great. Devin had seats for all of us on the side of the court. The athletic director came and talked to me, "Do you know," he asked, "how much your son could do for our program?" Elder Hales left his seat and came down to meet Devin. He said, "I just wanted to meet you." Devin has a sore back. We are praying for a recovery.

November 19, 1977. Went swimming with Devin in the evening. His back seems almost better now. I humbly pray that it is. It was fun to be with him.

November 26, 1977. Went to Devin's basketball game in the evening, Provo 92, Tooele 59. Devin's back was a little sore. He made 20 points and looked good. His team looks fantastic.

November 30, 1977. Devin played a great game tonight. Made 34 points against Viewmont. Coach Arnold was there.

December 2, 1977. Devin played tonight. His back was really paining him. I get so discouraged because I know how painful his back is. I pray with all my heart it will get better. It's so sad to see him at half speed. Jerry Pimm, Utah's coach called tonight. Devin wasn't home and I had a long talk with Coach Pimm about Devin's back. He said, "Mr. Durrant, Devin will be okay." It was the reassurance that I needed. I sure do like that guy.

5

Choosing Up Sides

"You're too little and you're too slow and
you can't catch good and we don't want you on our team!"
These words spoken to me by older brother Kent and sus-
tained by his friends nearly broke my heart. I ran straight to
my mother with a crying appeal for her to make Kent let
me play. Usually my tears about being mistreated caused
Mom to call him in and force him to stop persecuting me.

But this time she heard my sobbing story and to my surprise took no action against Kent. Instead she just continued mixing dough with her hands, which is what she was
doing when I had interrupted with my sad tale. As I
watched her she broke off a portion, rolled it out flat, and
cut it in small sections. She placed each piece in a pan of
hot grease and proceeded to fry delicious, golden brown
scones. Seeing the scones caused me to forget my heartbreak. She made enough for me. Then she kept making
more until she had a whole tin pan full. She handed me all
the scones and said, "Here, you take these and go outside

and see if they will play with you now." As soon as Kent and his friends spotted the scones, I heard the best words you can ever hear, "Hey, George, we want you on our team." Others quickly added, "Could we have a scone?" "Do you want to be captain?" "Could we have another scone?" I knew then the joy of being wanted, and I understood that the way to be chosen for any team was to have something to give.

As Devin was in his last year of high school, he had a whole pan of basketball scones to offer. Each college coach wanted him on his team. As they called to recruit him, I told the family, "I understand this recruiting business because I've been through it." They all looked amazed. I added, "When I played for the Sixth Ward, the Third Ward was always trying to get me to move over there. They offered me front row seats in church, free tickets to the Gold and Green Ball, and an invitation to attend their next potluck dinner without bringing anything. So I know about recruiting." The children were deeply impressed. At least I think they were.

I was a Regional Representative at the time when everyone wondered which college Devin would attend. At one stake conference I attended, the Stake President, LeLand Howell, got up at the beginning of the general session and said, "At this conference we are going to consider three great questions: Where did we come from? Why are we here? And most important where is Devin Durrant going?" Everybody laughed. But at the same time it was serious business because we were meeting in Orem. Everyone there wanted him to go to BYU. That's also where both Marilyn and I wanted him to go.

But where did Devin want to go? That was the big question. Many schools wanted to have him on their side. But we knew it would be either the University of Utah or BYU.

Each night we'd all gather around and talk about which college had called that day. I recall one Saturday the phone rang and I answered it.

A man said, "Mr. Durrant?"

I said, "Yes."

He said, "This is the coach of the University of Kentucky. As you know, Mr. Durrant, last year we won the national championship. We've lost four players. We just had a meeting with all the coaching staff and decided we are only going to bring in four new players. Your son is one of them. We want him here at the University of Kentucky. I just want to remind you we did win the national championship." He said he'd call back when Devin was home.

After I hung up I got to wishing I'd said, "Well, Coach, thank you for calling, but there is one thing you need to know."

He would have asked, "What's that?"

I'd have replied, "You see, Coach, I've never used my college eligibility — so wherever Devin plays, I want to play also."

I told the family that, and Marilyn, my adoring wife, chipped in her two cents worth and said, "Yes, and the coach would have said, 'We've heard about your ability, Mr. Durrant. We'd sooner have Devin's mom.' "

The next day Marilyn got a call. It was from Harvard. The man said, "Let me paint you a picture, Mrs. Durrant. It's four years from now. We're at the Harvard graduation. You and Mr. Durrant are sitting there watching your son as he comes up and walks across the stand. He's presented a diploma. He's graduated from Harvard. Wouldn't that be something, Mrs. Durrant, to have your son graduate from Harvard? Harvard is the finest university in America. Mrs. Durrant, we want your son to come back here and play basketball for us. We know he'll get many other offers, but he'll never get another chance to go to Harvard. People all over this country dream of their children going to Harvard. We get a thousand applicants for every student that gets to come here. We want your son. We'll expect him to come here and play basketball for us."

Marilyn of course was speechless at the time, but when she told us about it she acted as if she had been calm and collected.

Jerry Pimm was coaching at the University of Utah. Our family liked him a lot. He'd been in our home and talked to us many times. He knew each of us by our first name. When Devin was a junior in high school, Coach Pimm was the first one who said that Devin would be a college player.

Another reason why we liked coach Pimm was that we had had a special experience with him. As a high school senior, Devin had a bad back. He missed the first preseason game because he couldn't bear the pain of running and jumping. During the Pleasant Grove game he tried to play but was forced to retire to the bench. Following the game we all came home. After Devin and all the family had gone to bed, I was still up: I was so concerned about Devin that I could not sleep. I knelt down in the front room and prayed for him. Just as I finished, the phone rang. It was Jerry Pimm calling.

He said, "Hello, Mr. Durrant. I just called to see how things are going."

I said, "They are not going well."

He asked, "What's the matter?"

I replied, "Devin's back is getting worse."

He paused and then said, "I want to tell you something, Mr. Durrant. Devin's back is going to be okay, and don't you worry about it."

I asked, "How do you know that?"

He replied, "I just know."

With tears in my eyes and my voice breaking with emotion, I replied, "Coach Pimm, you've been an answer to my prayers, and I love you."

He said, "I love you too, Mr. Durrant."

That's the kind of relationship our family had with him.

We loved Frank Arnold, the head coach at BYU. When he came calling we all knew we had truly had an impressive figure in our home. He was a man of great dignity. He was the greatest recruiter we ever met. He was firm, yet friendly. He knew how to make believers of us all. He'd say, "Mr. and Mrs. Durrant, we'll make a basketball player out of Devin. More than that, we'll make a man out of him."

It was hard to know where Devin should go to school. He was enjoying being recruited here and there and everywhere. Sort of like a teenager with twenty-seven invitations to the Preference Ball.

Under all the pressure Marilyn became very nervous about what he would do. She felt he had to go to BYU. I held back and thought, "I'm not going to say much until it gets down to decision time. Then, if my input is needed, I'll make my appeal to Devin to go to BYU." I didn't want to waste my ammunition early, even though I could tell that he was seriously interested in the University of Utah. All his brothers and sisters told him that they wanted him to go to BYU.

One night just before the big decision had to be made, Devin was sleeping in his basement bedroom. Suddenly he was awakened by someone standing at this bedside. It was Marilyn, his mother. She couldn't sleep because of her concern for him. She was dressed in a white nightgown. Without any formal or informal introduction, she simply said, "Devin, you're going to go to BYU." Then she departed as quickly as she had come. The next day when Devin awoke and came to breakfast, he said, "Father, last night something strange happened. I don't know if it was the angel Moroni or someone else. All I know is that somebody appeared at my bedside and told me I had to go to BYU." Marilyn, who was stirring pancake batter, stirred even faster.

They say basketball players always go to the college where their mothers want them to go. So after that experience, wishing to disappoint neither an angel nor his mother, Devin decided to go to BYU.

Some folks have told us they don't like the recruiting that goes on, but we enjoyed it. We often laughed about it, and never took it too seriously. It wasn't a big crisis. We didn't mind the phone ringing and ringing. It gave our family something to talk about every night. Because of Devin we each felt as though we had a big pan full of scones.

Journal: December 1977–January 1978

December 6, 1977. Went to Salt Lake City where Devin and Provo played Highland. It was a classic game. The teams were fairly even. Devin had his best game of his career and that was the difference. He scored 39 points. He was unstoppable. Coach Pimm was there with his assistant. They were really impressed. We had a long talk with them after. The final score was 81 to 70. Needless to say we were exceedingly proud of Devin.

December 16, 1977. Provo defeated Springville tonight. Devin made 30 points. He got knocked down and looked hurt, but he got up and seemed to be all right. Everyone cheered.

December 17, 1977. Devin made 29 points tonight against Weber. He sure has fun while he plays. But he was discouraged after tonight's game. He comes home with us and doesn't seem to want to run around much with his friends.

December 23, 1977. Devin played against Payson tonight at Payson. He scored 37 points. They [Payson] only made 35 all together. It's sure fun to watch him play. He is smooth.

December 30, 1977. In the evening we went to Provo High gym to watch Devin play. He scored 37 points in just three quarters. He makes the game appear to be pure joy.

January 2, 1978. Devin is in Salt Lake City to see Utah play. He had a long talk with Coach Arnold today. He told Devin that the coach of North Carolina felt Devin was the best man at the prestigious San Diego Super Star Summer Camp.

January 4, 1978. Devin cut his hand on the rim of the basket in practice. Five or six stitches. I don't know if he will be able to play on Friday. He felt quite ill tonight.

January 5, 1978. Devin made 45 points against Orem. Many college coaches there.

January 13, 1978. Devin and his team played Dixie in the evening. Devin made 34 points. He didn't have a good game. Nevertheless, we sure have fun after the game talking to him. He almost always comes right home after the games. He is a great son.

6

The Sportsmanship Trophy

When they remodeled my old chapel, they removed the trophy case. They gave me one of the trophies. My children asked, "What's the trophy for, Pops?" With great pride I said, "Let me tell you how we won this. I played for my ward. We had a fine team that year. I'd grown some after high school and was playing pretty good. We had a coach named Ira Taylor who didn't know much about basketball, but he loved us. He and I talked often about things that matter a lot.

"Our team had a meeting before the regional tournament. We decided we wouldn't say anything to the referee other than good things. We even decided we wouldn't even think bad things about the referees. We prayed before each game for the strength to do what we'd decided. We almost won the tournament. The people watching sensed that we were a little different than the other teams. After the final game, the team that won the tournament got the championship trophy. Another team won consolation.

Then they chose the most outstanding player and gave him a wrist watch.

"Last of all the announcer said, 'Now for the most prestigious award of all—the sportsmanship trophy.' My heart pounded as I waited. 'It goes to the American Fork Sixth Ward. George Durrant, captain of the Sixth Ward team, come down and get this trophy for your team.'

"All the eyes were on me. I stepped down from one bleacher seat to the next. It seemed like I was flying. I walked out about ten paces. The man shook my hand and gave me the trophy. Everybody applauded. I held the trophy above my head. Then I held it close to my heart. I sure was happy."

I concluded that great story by saying, "I'll always remember winning that sportsmanship trophy. I know that sometimes we laugh and joke about sportsmanship trophies. But that was the highlight of my sports career."

Recently at a game I could see that my son Mark was upset. As he ran down the court, he glared at an opposing player. A few minutes later a foul was called on the man guarding Mark. The opponent quickly turned to the referee and shouted, "Come on, Ref. He moved into me."

Mark responded, "Quit whining."

A minute later a technical foul was called on a player on Mark's bench. While the referee was explaining the reason for the technical to the scorekeepers, Mark took the ball and rolled it down to the opposite end of the court. The referee didn't see what had happened, but the opposing coach did and told the referee to call another technical.

The next night Mark and I drove over to the Smith Fieldhouse. Mark was shooting foul shots, and I was shagging the ball for him.

I said, "You were a bit upset last night, weren't you?"

"Yeah, I kind of lost it, didn't I, Dad?"

"You sure did."

"My friend Blake really got on me after the game."

"I sure hope you can avoid acting that way in the future."

"Hey, Dad, don't worry about it. All I'm doing is being competitive."

"No, son. You're doing a lot more than being competitive. Last night you were acting pretty foolish."

"Yeah, I was, wasn't I. I'll try to do better, Pops."

"Thanks, son. That sure would mean a lot to me."

While we were engaged in that conversation, Mark hit twenty out of twenty free throws.

There sure is something good that can happen when there is a dad, a boy, and a ball. We talked heart-to-heart in the gym. Such a talk would have been a bit more difficult anywhere else.

I used the word *foolish* to describe Mark's unsportsmanship behavior. Perhaps the word *stupid* is a more descriptive word. I know that word is a bit harsh, but when you see some athletes carry on out on the field or the court you can't really describe their actions with any other word.

I recall a discussion our family had on sportsmanship. We were talking about who would go to the telestial kingdom, who would go to the terrestrial kingdom, and who would go to the celestial kingdom.

We decided you'd go to the kingdom that would best mirror the way you lived and acted while on earth. We talked about truth versus lies, kindness versus cruelty, helping versus hurting, love versus hate. Then I said, "Sportsmanship versus unsportsmanship." That got us going. Some of the boys who had been hoping the family home evening would soon be over suddenly were totally involved.

Dwight said, "If you have to be a good sport to get to the celestial kingdom, I'll tell you somebody who isn't going." He continued, "I was up at the stake center last night and Brother So-and-so was insulting the referee all night. Then he threatened to punch a guy from the other ward."

I replied, "Come on. Brother So-and-so wouldn't do that. He is as nice a guy as I've ever met."

"I know," Dwight replied. "I was shocked at the way he acted."

I said, "Sounds like he was acting a bit telestial."

"That's right," Dwight said. "He was out of control. He was not acting like he does in other aspects of his life. He was ranting and raving, complaining about every call, getting angry at the guy guarding him and shouting at him or wanting to punch him. Then, to cap it off, he acted the same way even after the game. He told the referee that he had never seen anyone, anywhere, anytime, as incompetent as he was."

I replied, "Well, that's a good description of telestial behavior. Now let's describe a terestrial player."

Devin responded, "That would be where the game was really tight. You go up for a shot and you are fouled. The ref doesn't call it. You look at him and say, 'Come on, Ref. Are you blind? He nearly tore my arm off!' But then after the game you would say, 'Hey, Ref, nice game. Sorry about my little outburst.' "

"Celestial—what's that?" I asked.

"That's me," said mother Marilyn.

"Come on," I said jokingly. "The way you act at BYU games, you hover toward the low end of terrestrial."

She quickly replied, "I just want BYU to win. That's why I shout, 'Kill them, kill them!' Besides," she said, "the president of the university says that he likes the way I cheer. He says that because of his position he can only shout, 'Show them no mercy. Show them no mercy.' "

Matt added, "Mom is doing better since you got her that score book. She's so busy charting field goals attempted, field goals made, assists, and rebounds that she can hardly do any shouting. That was an inspired idea, getting that book."

"I guess celestial," I said, "is to play the game in the name of Jesus Christ. In other words, play it the way he would."

"That's hard to do," Dwight said. "You get all excited and almost before you know it you shout something at another player or at the ref."

"Sure," I said, "But then you get hold of yourself and turn the other cheek. Then at a pause in the action you can say, 'I'm sorry.' "

"As fans we need to do the same thing," added Marinda.

"You're right, Marinda, but you never shout anything when your team is playing and losing, you just start to cry."

In summary I said, "I guess it's sometimes hard to be celestial on the court or field. But we can make sure we are at least terrestrial. Let's never rant and rave and act stupid, or, I should say, act telestial."

That night might have been the most religious sports discussion of all time. Sports is a subject that can lubricate many good gospel discussions.

In a talk that Devin gave, he told a story about a collegiate referee. Before the game, this wonderful official called the players around him at the center circle. He said, "During the game you players are going to make some bad plays and we refs are going to make some bad calls. When these things happen, let's just go on with the game."

In the second half Devin was driving for a lay-up. He was knocked to the floor. While he was lying there flat on his back, the referee came over. Devin looked up with a pleading look in his eyes. The ref pointed his finger down at him and shouted, "Charging." Looking up, Devin smiled and said, "Ref, you sure were right. You said before the game you were going to make some bad calls, and you just made one." The referee laughed but he didn't change the call. Of all the basketball stories Devin ever told me, the ones I liked the best were the ones about his relationship with the referees.

My firsthand knowledge about being a poor sport started when I was a preteenager out on my home court in the barn. It was there that I first felt the real pain of personal defeat. My brother, four years older than me, came out to the barn. Foolishly he challenged me to a game on my home court. As we got under way, I was playing better than I'd ever played. I was hitting long shot after long shot. I wasn't keeping score, but I knew that I had him down by ten or more. I was therefore shocked when he announced that the score was tied and that whoever made the next basket was the winner. The trouble was that just as he said what he did he had the ball and was right under the basket. I lunged to get to him to block his shot but I was too late. The ball came down through the basket, and he declared himself the national champ.

I was beside myself with anger and frustration. I shouted, "You didn't win. I made more points than you." He laughed as he headed out of the barn door. I looked around to get some other witnesses, and there was the cow with her head reaching through the stall trying to get some more hay. I made my appeal to her. She just kind of shrugged her shoulders as if to say, "Don't ask me, I can't count." I was in such anguish that I broke out in tears. As my brother headed toward the house, I shouted, "I won and you know it." He shouted back, "No way. I'm the champ."

I didn't know what to do. I thought surely the world had come to an end.

I guess I was really a sore loser in those days, because of what I did next. You see, he had a new baseball mitt that he had just bought with his own money. I saw it laying on the hay. He had forgotten to take it back into the house. In despair I picked it up, looked at it real close, and then flipped it over my shoulder into the pig pen. Then I walked slowly and dejectedly back into the house.

When I got there his first words were, "Hey, everybody, I beat George. I beat George." Then he said, "Oh, I forgot my mitt," and with that he headed out of the back door for the barn. While he was gone I sat staring silently out of our front window. After what seemed like an extra long time, he came in the back door and asked, "What did you do with my mitt?"

I said without hesitation, "I threw it out of the barn into the pig pen."

"You did what?" he shouted as he took off like a shot out of a cannon. Pretty soon he came back, holding the mitt kind of delicately with his thumb and one finger. The pigs hadn't eaten it, but they'd made it so nobody else would ever want to eat it either. I remember him as he held that mitt in front of me. With tears gathering in his eyes, he asked, "See what you've done. Now are you happy?"

I thought for a little while, and then I said, "Yeah, I am." But that was a lie. I wasn't happy. You never are happy when you're a bad sport, when you're a bad loser. It's okay to be a sad loser but not a bad loser.

At the final judgment when all the awards are given out, our family may not get the Most Handsome award, or the Most Intelligent award, or the Most Exciting award, or the Most Outstanding award. But I sure hope we'll be one of the families who will get a sportsmanship trophy. Because that is a trophy which is only found in the celestial kingdom.

Journal: January 1978–February 1978

January 15, 1978. Devin had phone calls tonight from Louisville and U of U.

January 18, 1978. Coach Pimm and Jeff Judkins came for three hours tonight. They want Devin at the U.

January 20, 1978. Went back to my old home town (American Fork) to watch Devin play. He played a superb game, 41 points. A real close game. Coaches were there from Arizona State, Utah, BYU, Weber. It was a night to remember forever. As a graduate of Utah's greatest school, I sang my school song, "Dear Old American Fork High," with great gusto.

January 27, 1978. Devin had 33 points against Pleasant Grove in a game at Provo.

February 1, 1978. When Devin came home, he said, "I've got some news that will make you happy."

He continued, "I'm going to Washington, D.C., the last of March and then on to Philadelphia. Coach Spencer, the greatest coach in America, is going with me." I asked, "What's the deal?" He said, "I'm going to play in the McDonald's All-American game and in the East-West All-Star Game." I was elated. This means that he is an all-American. I can't believe all this is happening to Devin. We had a good talk tonight about the past. About when he first discovered that he was a basketball player. We talked about Kentucky. We talked about how the Lord has blessed him so much. Devin said that he will do all that he can to promote the Lord's work.

So it is quite a thrill to be the father of an all-American. But it's even better to be the father of a number one young man. But it's still hard to believe. I'm sure it will bring some stress to Devin. But I feel he can handle it. Life is good. I love the Lord with all my heart and soul.

7

The Consolation Trophy

A Little League coach told me a story about winning. He said, "We had a game yesterday and I let all the boys play. One boy who's not much of an athlete played out in left field. After the game he came running up to me and asked, 'Did we win, did we win?' I asked. 'Did you get to play?' And he said, 'Yeah, I got to play,' and I said, 'Did you have fun?' And he said, 'Yeah, I had fun.' I replied, 'Then we won.' "

When you lose, if you search into life's total picture, you can find some consoling reason to rejoice. I have a young friend named Byrd; he comes from Barstow, California. He told me that the McDonald's in Barstow burned to the ground. A week or so later Barstow played Victorville in basketball. The game was played in Victorville but Barstow won. During the final minutes when they knew they were going to lose, the Victorville students began chanting, "We've got a McDonald's! We've got a McDon-

ald's!'' The consolation of knowing they had something
Barstow didn't helped the Victorvillians feel like winners.

During Devin's junior year in high school, Provo High's
undefeated Bulldogs had been rated number one all season. Skyline, who had won the tournament the year before, had lost only one game—that coming on a night
when a player named Danny Vranes had the flu and
couldn't play. Danny Vranes was the best to ever play prep
ball in Utah. In the state tournament we knew it would be a
mighty battle between Provo and Skyline. The two power-
houses met in the semifinals. It was generally felt that whoever won this game would win the next day and become
the state champion.

I went to the Special Events Center and took my seat. I
nervously watched as the players warmed up. I thought to
myself, "Before a game, the players on each team are winners. After the game, only half of them are."

During the first few minutes Provo wasn't playing up to
par. Soon they had fallen behind and their chances of winning appeared hopeless. But in the last quarter Provo began
to come back. Then, with just a few seconds to go, they
were only down by two points. A Provo player shot and
missed; Devin tipped the ball once and missed; he tipped it
again and missed, tipped it again and missed, tipped it again
and it went in. I'd never seen him jump like that before.

Now the score was tied. I was beside myself with excitement and anxiety. But it was Skyline's ball and they had
a chance to win. They came down the court cautiously,
passing the ball around. With about twenty seconds to go,
the ball came to the hands of one of their best shooters. Because it wasn't an unusually long shot, he must have felt
confident he could make it. He shot. The ball bounced
around and fell out.

Provo grabbed the rebound and immediately called
time out. There were fourteen seconds to go. During the
time out, I had time to think, to pray, to dream, and to
hope. I also had time to tremble. Time was now in. Provo
High came down the court. One last shot and they would
win it. Even if they missed they'd tie. Suddenly with seven

seconds to go, Greg Baliff got the ball and spotted a clear lane to the basket. As he was about to make a lay-up Danny Vranes stepped out in front of him and he couldn't go any farther. It was still a short shot. Greg was deadly from that range. He put it up. The ball rolled around and came out. Danny Vranes pulled down the rebound and called time out with three seconds left.

We waited again. It was now Skyline's chance to win. Surely three seconds was not enough time for them to score. A Skyliner took the ball out of bounds at the far end of the court and threw it into a fellow named Slaymaker who was blindingly fast. He took several quick dribbles down court and threw the ball to Danny Vranes at the outer edge of the foul circle. Danny didn't even look. If he'd looked I would have felt better about it, but he didn't even look. He just jumped and turned into the air and shot. While the ball arched toward the hoop, the game ended. A second later the ball nestled in the net. Skyline had won, and Provo and my son had lost.

The Skyline winners were jumping around and shouting. Their fans were embracing each other. I, one of the losers, was stunned. I thought the world had come to an end. There was no way I could go on, no way I could continue to live. I couldn't take it any longer. I headed for the door.

That night when we got home, there was complete gloom at our house. I sat at the kitchen table. Marilyn was cooking dinner; I didn't want to talk about the game. Just then the door flew open. It was Devin. He threw his green and white athletic bag in front of the closet door. He turned to his right and entered the kitchen. I didn't want to look at him. I knew his heart was broken. The thing I dreaded most since we had lost the game two hours before was talking to him. I knew that my grief would be multiplied ten times by his sad heart. To my surprise he shouted, "Hello, Pops, what's going on? Is dinner about ready?" I lifted my head. I knew that his sorrow at losing ran deep, but he was determined to console all of us. He spoke again, "Hey, Pops, don't be sad. It's just a game.

We'll get them next year." Just those trite words gave me consolation. I stood up, looked into his eyes, and could feel his inward pain. All I could say was, "I'm sorry."

He joined us all at his usual place at our round table. We had a short prayer and started to eat. The phone rang. It was a friend calling. He reported that while listening to the radio he had heard Jerry Pimm say that he liked the way Devin played and that Devin and Fred Roberts each had a great chance to play college ball. Those words from an expert brought us joy. We talked about the future as we continued to eat.

By dessert time we were no longer talking about basketball. Our conversation had evolved to just talking about our family. Kathryn got up from her seat, went behind Devin, and massaged his tired shoulders. We all moved our chairs close together. We decided to pray. We thanked the Lord for our family and the blessings of living together in love. We thanked him for Devin and for his successes. Most of all we thanked him for the gospel which gave our lives direction. After the prayer we sat and talked some more. The Spirit of the Lord was with us. It was as if we were totally surrounded with blessings. That night was the sweetest night our family ever spent together. We had lost the game but once again we had won each other's love. Besides that, we had a McDonald's.

The next year it was Provo High against Box Elder in the state championship game. Box Elder wasn't supposed to give Provo High a game at all, but they did. Provo would score and then Box Elder would score. I should say, Devin would score and then Box Elder would score. Devin would score and Box Elder would score. Finally with just a few seconds to go, Provo was ahead by two points. Box Elder came down and needed to score to tie it. With about fifteen seconds to go they shot. The ball rolled around and fell out. Their tallest player tipped it up, and again it fell out. Another tipped it. Again it missed. Finally the ball went out of bounds. A Provo player had touched it last. Box Elder threw it in and their best shooter shot from the corner. The ball rolled around and fell out. The game ended. Provo High had won.

Now the Provo High winners were the heroes who were jumping around like Skyline's had done the year before. Box Elder was in a state of remorse. As we drove home that night we were too excited to talk. We went out to a restaurant, where we ate pie and ice cream. It was wonderful to be a winner, but there was not anything special about that night for our family.

Oh, sure we felt we were maybe a little bit better than other people because our team had won. We had the kind of pride that comes through winning. It's an excited sort of inward feeling. But it's very different from the feeling you get when you lose.

I'm not complaining—I'd still rather be a winner than a loser. Yet something wonderful can happen when you lose. I have found that those same feelings come when I lose at any of life's endeavors. Losing can bring feelings of love and humility which cause me to regroup, to count my blessings, and to go back to work. It isn't harmful to your soul to occasionally taste defeat.

Mark, my youngest son, plays for Provo High. Of him I wrote in my journal: "Tomorrow night Provo and Spanish Fork are matched in the first round of the state tournament. It worries me greatly.

"I won't be able to go to the game because of a commitment I made long ago. I could listen to the first part of it on the radio, but I don't think I will. To listen to part and then have to leave would be more than I could bear. I try to pray for victory. But because I know the players from the other team, I can't mention my son without mentioning Randy Reid and their great players. All I can do is pray that my son does his best.

"I keep telling myself that whether we win or lose, life goes on. Things that really matter remain the same. But try as I will, I can't put out of my mind the thoughts of the game and the hope for victory and the fear of defeat.

"Tonight at family home evening, Mark and Marilyn

and I didn't talk much about the tournament. We talked about other things. We sat close together and hoped and prayed that all things, in all matters, would go well. Mark seems to be calm even though he sings a lot. Perhaps he is like me. I tend to sing or whistle when I'm a bit nervous.''

The next night I wrote: "This morning Mark talked endlessly to our little dog, Skoshie. So I'm sure he is nervous. When he left for school he was dressed in a shirt and tie and a blue sports coat. He looked handsome. We had our morning prayer. I prayed again that he would do well. I told him, 'All the best to you, my son.' He went to school and I went to work.''

The next day I wrote: "The game was played last night. I went to a meeting where I had to be. From time to time during the meeting, I thought of the game that was being played at that very time and I wondered and I worried.

"I recorded the game at home. After the meeting I hurried home and turned on the tape recorder. No one was home but me. All the family was at the game. I listened only briefly to parts of the game. Then I turned the tape ahead to the last minute. Spanish Fork was ahead by two points with just a few seconds to go. They had a one-and-one foul shot. One of the best players was shooting. I knew it was all over and the game was hopelessly lost. He missed the foul try, and Provo got the rebound with eighteen seconds to go. They came down and passed the ball to Brian Santiago. He was way beyond the three-point line. He shot a long bomb. It hit the dead center of the basket. I went out of control with excitement.

"I was jumping around in the bedroom and my little dog looked at me like I was crazy. There were seven seconds left. I pushed the tape so that it went ahead a little. Provo now had the ball out of bounds with two seconds. 'They've got this one won!' I shouted to Skoshie. Provo had won. I quickly turned the tape recorder off and ran out of the bedroom. I ran out into the street and danced around the block, my heart was pounding so fast. It seemed like a big huge monster had been lifted up off my back. I was sure Spanish Fork was going to win. I'd never been so sure of anything. Tonight we play Mountain Crest. They are not supposed to be as good as Spanish Fork. We'll see.

"I stayed at the Missionary Training Center tonight and gave my talk to the new missionaries. I felt a bit on edge after the meeting. I went out and listened to my car radio. Provo was down by ten points in the second half. As I listened, they caught up and went ahead by five. Then they fell behind again and lost. I just hadn't expected to lose today. Yesterday I had, but today I hadn't. Yesterday we won, today we didn't. Life is like that.

"Mark got home at about ten-thirty. We talked. He said, 'When I look at the future, all the tests I've got to take, another tournament, then my mission, I get a bit over-whelmed.' We talked about his heavy load in school. The coach wants Mark and his teammates to start getting up at six and practicing basketball. He'll probably be studying until eleven o'clock each night. It just seems a bit heavy. It's quite a thing for an athlete to give his all to sports and also try to be a scholar. As we talked Mark said, 'I guess it's time for me to grow up. I've been a kid long enough.' I told him, 'You've got to take it a day at a time.' We talked about his good sense of humor, his multitude of friends, and his family who all love him. I could tell he was tired and that his heart was heavy.

"It was near midnight. He said, 'Do you know what I really miss? I miss little Lexi and Ben' [his niece and nephew]. He added, 'They used to come and see us every day for a year. Now they don't come anymore because they are in Kentucky. I miss them more than I can ever say.' He and I nearly came to tears over that one. I told him, 'That's what really matters. Family and those kind of things. You'll play well in basketball and you'll do well in school and everything will turn out all right.' I asked him if he'd like a blessing and he said he would. By the power of the priesthood and in the name of Jesus Christ I blessed him. I told him that all would be well, that things would work out, that his mind should be at peace, that he should do the right thing, the friendly thing, the honorable thing, in every situation. During the blessing we both felt the Spirit of the Lord. I was able to tell him of my love for him and of his Heavenly Father's love for him. We embraced, said good night, and went to bed.''

I talked to one man once who said he'd like to eliminate competitive sports. He said he went to a place where his daughter had been playing volleyball. He got there late and people were coming out. He told me, ''I didn't even have to ask who won. I could tell by looking at the two groups of girls as they left. One group was in tears.'' He added, ''It's not right to do that to people.'' I silently thought, ''Sure it is. Losing's all right as long as you aren't really a loser. You're not a loser as long as you keep hurting whenever you lose. True losers are those who lose and then say, 'I don't care.' ''

Losing never dampened my enthusiasm for sports. Oh, it broke my heart a few times. But a few cracks in the heart never really hurt anybody. It just helps them to understand other people. Others have similar wounds. As a matter of fact, if sports does any harm at all, it's the harm it does to those that are always winning. Fortunately, you seldom find any winners that haven't had some heartbreaking losses somewhere along the line.

Matt was almost four years older than Devin. As children, the two of them were rivals even though Matt was always able to win. Once we went on a vacation up into Canada. Some people let us stay in a vacant house. One morning after we had been away from home for a week, I was in shaving. My son Matt came in and said, ''Dad, I want to go home.''

''Why? We're on vacation.''

He replied, ''Because I can't stand to be with the family anymore, and I want to catch a bus and go home and you go on.''

''What's the problem?'' I asked.

He replied, ''Devin.''

''What do you mean?'' I asked.

''He bothers me. I can't stand to be around him another minute.''

''What does he do?''

"Oh, he is always saying stuff and doing stuff and I just can't stand it. I want to go home; I just don't want to be around him."

I quit shaving and went and sat on the rug in the unfurnished front room and said, "Matt, go get Devin and let's talk." Devin came and sat by us. Matt was about thirteen at the time.

"Now, Matt, you tell Devin how you feel."

He said, "I don't want to tell him how I feel."

I said, "You tell him."

Matt hesitated and then with deep emotion said, "I want to go home."

Devin asked, "Why?"

Matt replied, "Because of you."

"Why?" Devin asked with tears flooding his eyes.

"Because I can't stand to be around you, that's why."

"Why can't you stand to be around me?"

Matt replied with a tone of spite, "Because you're always saying things and doing things. I can't stand you."

Then, after several seconds of silence, Devin softly spoke amidst his tears, "The reason why I always say stuff to you is that every time we play a game, you always win."

"Sure I win, 'cause I'm better than you."

"Yeah, but just remember that every time you win, I lose." Then Devin turned away to hide his tears.

Matt softened and said, "Well, if you won't say stuff to me then maybe we can work it out."

"I'd sure like that," I said. "We don't want you to go home, Matt." We all felt consoled as we sat and talked about winning and losing. But we knew we had all just won a big one and nobody had lost. A few minutes later we were all sitting in a McDonald's eating Egg McMuffins.

Journal: February 1978 – March 1978

February 3, 1978. Today I spoke at a forum assembly at the Salt Lake City Institute of Religion at the U of U. Coach Pimm and his staff and Danny Vranes and two Judkins brothers were there. They all came up after and we talked. Arnie Ferrin, the athletic director, and a vice-president of the University of Utah were also there. Suddenly I'm very important up there. They want Devin in the worst way. Tonight Provo 94, Timpview 49. Devin, 27 points in three quarters. He was fantastic. Coaches Arnold and Pimm were there, as were their teams. Had a conference with Coach Spencer and Arnold after the game. Trying to decrease pressure.

February 4, 1978. Devin had a long visit with Coach Arnold this morning at his coach's office. Coach Arnold is really worried that he will lose Devin. I feel Devin will go to the Y, but there sure are a multitude of rumors about his going to the U. Marilyn, Dwight, Sharon, Gene, and Devin all went to the Y-U game at the Y. Devin got us all tickets on the front row. The U won. I didn't mind because now that I know their coach and players I sort of like them.

February 15, 1978. Tonight all three TV channels had reports on Devin. His name is on the lips of many people. We had a good family home evening talking about his sudden rise to fame and all the interesting side effects. Many people are anxious to get in touch with us. Harvard called him tonight, as did Utah, BYU, and a sports announcer. I made a tape for Matt (who is in Japan on a mission), telling him of all the excitement. It's all like a dream.

February 18, 1978. Devin was invited today to play in the Kentucky Derby Classic. That is a game where the Kentucky and Indiana all-stars play against the United States all-stars. Devin had seen that game when he was in the ninth grade, and he dreamed then of someday playing in it. Marilyn and I may fly to Louisville to see him play and to visit our old home and friends. We love Louisville and Kentucky. Devin is sure getting some wonderful opportunities.

February 22, 1978. Coach Hall, from Kentucky, called today to ask Devin to come back to Kentucky and play. Vern Hatten, an old friend, also called recruiting for Kentucky.

February 27, 1978. His back is much better but it is still a problem. The Kentucky coaches called Devin and told him they are coming to his game at St. George.

March 1, 1978. Devin played ball in St. George tonight. He made 35 points in a tight game. The Kentucky assistant coach was there.

March 3, 1978. Marilyn and I had dinner with President and Sister Gardiner (president of U of U) in his office. Just the four of us. We were there one and one-half hours. He is a tremendous man. They of course invited us because they want Devin. We attended Devin's last high school game today. He scored 38 points against American Fork. It was a close game. Devin pulled it out in the end. His back still pains him a great deal. But he doesn't tell anyone. Harvard wrote Marilyn and me a great letter today. They sure seem to want Devin. I talked to Coaches Pimm and Arnold at the game. That's quite a battle.

March 4, 1978. Spent an hour in the morning visiting with Coach Arnold in his office. At his invitation. It was a most significant meeting. I believe him to be a man of high character. I'd love to have Devin play for him and associate with him. Tonight Devin and I had a good talk. He told me of a recent seminary leadership meeting for which he was responsible. He was more excited about that than about basketball. We listened to a tape of some of last night's radio broadcast of the American Fork game.

March 7, 1978. Tonight the coach of Kentucky — the number one team in the nation — called. He said that they had a coaching staff meeting today. They were thinking about ten recruits. But they only have four scholarships. They decided on the four players they want, and Devin is one of them. He said that that is really big news in Kentucky. He will call back and talk to Devin.

March 15, 1978. Devin and Provo defeated Logan tonight 60 to 53 in the state tournament. It was quite a close game. Devin did well—he had 24 points.

March 17, 1978. Provo beat Murray today. I was afraid that they wouldn't. But I had a sort of impression that they would.

March 18, 1978. This is one of those days that will never be forgotten. I have a deep feeling that this entire script was written in heaven. It seems someone up there has singled out Devin and pointed a finger of fame at him. I believe the Lord is blessing him in a special way for a purpose. Devin has really caught the fancy of the entire state. His name is on the lips of everyone. Anyway, Provo won the state championship. It was on TV. Devin was fantastic and scored 38 points. Final score 52–50. Box Elder was so very hot in their shooting. The two teams traded baskets the entire game. The finish was breathtaking. It was so exciting that the entire crowd and TV audience was in awe. The celebration that followed was indescribable. Devin held the trophy high above his head and led his team around the gym. He was interviewed on TV. I hugged Devin after the game. Our young daughter, Marinda, cried. Coach Spencer, the greatest coach alive, was as happy as a man ever could be. We drove home. We went to a cafe with the coaches and the team. We ate pie. It was very late. I finally was in bed but could not sleep. Never have I been so excited.

8

The Championship Trophy

One of the great philosophical questions of the day is "Sir, would you choose Hamburger A, a Wendy's hamburger that is made fresh, or Hamburger B, made earlier so that it's dry?"

An even better question is "Would you choose Life A, a championship way of living that will bring you joy, or Life B, one that will make you a loser?"

It is amazing how many people choose Life B.

Another great question often asked in our day is "How are you?" If we reply with an unenthusiastic, "Fine," it sounds as if we have chosen Life B, the dry and empty one. If we have chosen Life A we are certainly better than fine.

I have made it a policy to never reply to the question, "How are you?" with the answer, "Fine." Instead, I often say, "Champion." My son, Devin, has given me a nickname. He calls me that name often. Yet each time I get a thrill when he sees me and says, "Hello, Champ." Oh, how I'd like to be worthy to be called "Champ!"

Does the Lord care about the final score of the championship game? I think not. But at the same time he cares
about us. And we care about games. So I still don't know
whether we should pray that our team will win.

I remember once when BYU beat Notre Dame in a great
national televised game in the NCAA tournament. I've been
told that Jeffrey Holland, president of BYU, came to the
Cougar dressing room just before the players were to take
the floor. Normally the pregame prayers were that the team
members would play their best, that no one would be in-
jured, and so on. But I've been told that at that exciting
moment, Jeffrey Holland prayed that BYU, the decided
underdog, would win. I'm not sure that BYU won because
of the prayer as much as because of the last-second basket
by Danny Ainge.

When we lived in Kentucky, Devin's Seneca High
School ninth-grade team was playing a crucial game. There
were only a few fans on the north end of the bleachers
cheering for Seneca, and a few in the south end cheering
for the other team. Regulation play ended in a tie. During
the first overtime each team scored six points. During the
second overtime Devin scored most of the points for his
team. The score changed hands several times and was tied
with just three seconds to go. The small but vocal crowd
was in a frenzy. A teammate passed the ball to Devin. He
jumped and shot over the hand of the defender. As the ball
arched toward the basket, time in the game ran out. The
shot looked on target but was just an inch or so too long. It
hit the back of the rim and rebounded to the foul line.

My disappointment changed to hope when I realized
that a foul had been called. The referee said that the foul
was right after the shot—Devin would get to shoot a one-
and-one. I sat there looking at my son, who could now win
the game if he could just make his first free throw.

I decided that I shouldn't pray about the foul shot. Just
as the ref was about to hand Devin the ball, the other team
called time out. I was beside myself with anxiety. I considered again whether I should pray. Again I decided
against it. Both teams came back out on the court, and the

referee was about to hand Devin the ball. My heart pounded within my chest as I wondered, "Should I pray? No," I said to myself, "I shouldn't." I glanced down to the other end of the gym. The opposing fans there were leaning forward with their eyes focused on my son. I was sure they were praying that Devin would miss.

By now Devin had the ball. Again I was tempted to pray, but again I didn't. His knees were bending, he held the ball in position, and finally he shot. Just as the ball left his hand I couldn't restrain myself: I cried out with a silent appeal, "Oh, dear Heavenly Father, let it go in." A second later the ball was in the net. I bounded out of the stands with total excitement. I embraced my young son and told him that I loved him.

I still don't know whether I should have prayed for that foul shot to go in. But I do know, and I will always know, that it's right to pray, for a son or a daughter. In circumstances such as this basketball game, the answer to the prayer is not as important as the fact that a prayer was said. I quickly admit that since that day in Kentucky I've prayed for the success of other shots, some of which turned out to be airballs.

Losing can bring deep sorrow. But out of that soil of sorrow can grow compassion and understanding.

I remember sitting on the bench during my high school basketball career. My friends would sometimes shout, "Put old George in!" That was about as humiliating as things can get. I'd silently appeal to the Lord to inspire the coach to put me in. That's when I first found out the Lord didn't care who won a game, because he didn't prompt the coach to put me in. If I'd gone in we'd have won for sure.

Instead I stayed on the bench. At the time I didn't think the Lord heard my prayers. Now I know that he did because while I was sitting there on the bench I found out how it feels to sit on the bench. It was in that sad soil that my life's philosophy grew. From those losing experiences, I learned about true religion. I decided to go around looking for people who are sitting on benches. Then, knowing how they feel, I asked them to stand up. When they asked,

"What do you care?" I answered, "I care because I know how you feel, and I love you. Now, come on, let's go, let's get up and get going."

When a player loses a game of basketball or any contest of life, especially when he put his whole heart into it, he is often ready to hear the words of the Apostle Peter: "Rise up and walk." Walk toward character, compassion, understanding, and love.

When we play well on our homecourt, when we follow the example of real heroes, when we have a "scone" in our heart for everyone we meet, when we win the sportsmanship trophy, when we have dignity in victory or defeat, then we will look up at life's scoreboard and see that we deserve the title "the Champ."

Journal: March 1978 – April 1978

March 27, 1978. There continues to be an intense interest in where Devin will go to school. He left for Washington, D.C., today. Coach Spencer and Mrs. Spencer went with him.

April 7, 1978. Devin went to the *Deseret News* all-state banquet tonight. He was chosen 3A MVP. Coach Spencer was selected the Coach of the Year.

April 10, 1978. I sat down to write Matt a letter. As I was writing Devin came upstairs. He said, "Start a new paragraph, Dad, and tell Matt that Devin is going to be a Cougar." I stood up and embraced him. I was filled with joy. So the long wait is over. He put on his new navy blue suit and went up to tell Coach Arnold the news. Coach Arnold was of course pleased. From that moment on the news spread rapidly. I'm grateful to the Lord for his decision.

April 28, 1978. At nine o'clock we went to Freedom Hall, in Louisville, Kentucky, to watch Devin and the U.S. all-stars practice. Devin looked good, as did the entire fabulous team.

April 29, 1978. Back to Freedom Hall at ten o'clock in the morning to see the one-on-one contest. I wanted Devin to at least win his first round. He did. I thought, if he could also win his second round that would be so satisfying. He did. And he won again and again until he had beaten some of the most talented high school players in America. Then he was in the finals. He won again and suddenly there he was — "The Champion." The announcer and others made much of the fact that he had learned to play the game in Louisville.

Back to Freedom Hall at seven. We were seated on the end of the playing floor just behind the basket. I made a tape recording upon which I did a play-by-play of the game so that I could send it to Matt in Japan. Devin played well. He did some quite amazing things. I was thrilled with his performance. He looked so good on the court before the 16,000 fans who filled all the seats. A great game. Quite close. Devin hit a jump shot in the late moments. Then another, then another. Suddenly his team was up by five points. The U.S. team won 132 to 127. After the game the most valuable player award was given. Devin had a slight chance. But surely he wouldn't win. Public address man: ". . . And the Most Valuable Player award goes to Devin Durrant." I went almost out of my mind with glee. It had been such an impossible dream. But he had done it. He had done it in Louisville before his old friends and before the many Mormons who were in the hall.

A Dad, a Boy, a Ball, and a Call

The sports pages have captured much of Devin's career, but what follows here is the rest and by far the more important part of the story.

Journal: November 1978–April 1984

November 5, 1978. Talked to Bishop Douglas this morning about Devin's future mission call. He said that he had asked if Devin could go in the spring of '79. That way he could get back and have several months to get ready for the '82 season. But because Devin won't be

nineteen until the fall of '79, the bishop was told that
Devin couldn't go until fall. Devin had told the bishop if
that is the case he will stay and play all four years before
his mission. I sure don't feel that that would be the thing
to do. At five o'clock, Devin, Matt, and Kathryn came
up. We went over to the church. The bishopric and high
councilors were there. I then had the great honor of
ordaining Devin an elder. I've never had a greater spiritual thrill. He has a bright future.

   November 23, 1978. Went to Marriott Center at six
o'clock. I've never been more excited or more thrilled
than I was when the band played "Rise and Shout the
Cougars Are Out." During that inspiring song Devin
came onto the floor for his first college game. Some
22,000-plus fans were watching, and I was the most
proud of all. He scored the first point of the season with
a foul pitch. He went on to score 13 points. The Y
looked great and won 95 to 60. When the game started I
was so nervous I was trembling. It's wonderful to be
able to do something yourself, but to see a son or
daughter do it brings far more joy than doing it yourself.

   November 24, 1978. Devin started again in the
season's second game. I was a little more calm, but I was
still too nervous to talk to anyone before the opening
tipoff. He sure was happy after the game. He made 15
points. The fans seem to like him and all the rest of the
team. Final score: 111–80. We attended a party at Frank
Arnold's after the game. All the team and their parents
were there. We ate and watched some of the game on
TV.

   December 6, 1978. Devin played well and got 10
points. BYU won 99–80 over Utah State.

   December 9, 1978. The game started at nine.
Devin played well the first half in a tight game with
Purdue. In the second half he became devastating. He
was better than he had ever been. In that half he scored
20 points and had 26 all together. He made a slam dunk
to end the game. Devin was all over the court. He faked
and drove. The people were on fire with enthusiasm

about his play. I had wondered up until tonight just how well Devin would do in college. Tonight he showed me that he could be an all-American. He was interviewed on the radio after the game. Devin asked me how I felt. I replied, "My love for you is always constant, but my pride goes up and down. Right now it is at an all-time high." Devin was happy.

December 24, 1978. We opened a few gifts. It is hard to imagine anyone being happier than we were this night. Devin talked much about basketball and answered all of our questions. Later, as I retired, he came and laid on the bed with me and we talked. I asked him if he felt he would get better as a player. He replied that he felt that he would. I asked him about pro ball and he said that he'd sooner be married and have a family and just work. But he did feel it would be a good way to earn some money. I asked about a mission. He said he'd just have to wait and see. He wanted to go right after this season but he won't be nineteen until fall and the Brethren say he can't go until then. So he will wait at least until after his sophomore year and perhaps longer. It was good to talk to him. He is truly a good man. I feel the Lord will bless him and open the way for him to go on a mission at the right time.

December 29, 1978. Listened to the radio broadcast of Devin's game. He started and did fairly well but was taken out early in both the first and second halves. I feel he will have a struggle holding on to his starting position. BYU beat Houston.

January 4, 1979. Went to Devin's game tonight at Provo. He played very well. He is smooth. He got 16 points in a little over half the game. The Y won by some 40 points.

January 6, 1979. In a game with Utah State Devin had a great first half and scored 18 points. In the second half he did not score. Utah State won by quite a ways. He cheered me up on the long drive home. We talked much about his future.

January 11, 1979. BYU defeated UTEP by 25 points. Devin really played well and made 18 points. He was high-point man. He is getting better each game.

January 20, 1979. Went to U of U at six. Didn't sleep much last night because I was so nervous about the Utah game. But the game turned out well. BYU played nearly perfect ball. Devin did well. He made 15 points and no mistakes. BYU 90, Utah 75. I've never been happier about a sports victory. Devin came home with us and we had a family party.

January 25, 1979. Watched Devin and BYU play on TV against Colorado State. He hit 11 of 13 shots and BYU won. It is fun to both win and have Devin do well. There is much interest in whether he will go on a mission. Everyone has much advice to offer about that. Some say go. Some say no. All eyes seemed to be focused on him.

January 27, 1979. We listened to BYU play Wyoming on the radio. I had a feeling that we would lose and we did. Devin had a good game. He scored 19 points but he missed a few fouls at the end that could have won it. It went into overtime before they won 71 to 69. I really felt heartsick. But if you follow sports you have to be ready to accept defeat at times. As a matter of fact as painful as defeat is, it abounds in lessons which the soul needs. I get closer to the Spirit in defeat than in victory.

January 28, 1979. Last night after the Wyoming loss I spent a semi-sleepless night. Over and over there came into my mind how the game could have come out differently. My head seemed to almost be an echo chamber for the words, "Devin Durrant! Devin Durrant! Devin Durrant! Athlete! Missionary!" I got up and knelt down and prayed for peace of mind. Finally sleep came and with it a dream. I felt peace as I dreamed that I walked through a supermarket with Devin. Every person there came to Devin, each in a most reverent manner told of the great joy they felt in being able to meet him and shake his hand. Seeing that in my dream brought me deep joy and peace. When I awoke I had much reassurance that Devin had a bright future.

January 30, 1979. I continued to have little else on my mind but Devin going on a mission in the spring. After consulting with Devin I've asked the Brethren if an exception could be made so that he could go before being nineteen years old. I decided to pray about it. I had no sooner begun to pray when the phone rang. It was a staff member from the Missionary Department. I told him of my feelings about Devin and the desire to go early. As we talked I could tell that he understood. But he also let me know the pressures that would come from other parents if they ever heard that an athlete had been allowed to go early. He told me that the policy is that he must be nineteen. I told him I'd relay that message to Devin so he could decide if he wanted to go in the fall. I left my office with an urgent desire to talk to Devin.

January 31, 1979. I drove from Salt Lake City to Provo in the hopes of being able to find Devin. While I was parked in front of a restaurant, Devin drove up. It was another little miracle. He shouted some encouraging words to me and I got in the car with him. He was headed for basketball practice. Just being with him a few minutes lifted my spirits. As he went in the Marriott Center to dress for practice I walked down to campus. I visited my dear friend Paul Felt. He said, "Devin sure has the Spirit of the Lord with him." I returned to the practice. It was long and hard. Coach Arnold got upset that there wasn't enough hustle. After the practice I went to the training table dinner with Devin and his teammates. I had a great time there with all the players. After dinner I sat in the Cannon Center on a couch with Devin and we had a long and most inspiring talk. I told him of how at the recent farewell of Steve Motskus I could think of nothing but Devin and his mission. I told him that at that farewell I had a strong impression that the Lord desired him to go this fall. I said, "I don't want to bring pressure on you." He said, "Dad, if the Lord is speaking to you, I want to know what he is saying." I told him of all my feelings. I said things such as, "You can't be an example to young boys if you don't do what they are asked to do." He replied, "Dad, I love those kids." He told me of a birthday party he went to for a nine-year-old and his friends. He told of how they looked at him and how they just wanted to be near him. He said, "I never want to let those kids down." We grew closer and closer as we talked. He said, "I hate to let my teammates down." I told him that if he decides to go he should tell the coach within a week. That shocked him as he felt that after the season would be soon enough. I pointed out that Coach Arnold needed to know soon so that he could recruit a forward.

Devin said he would like a chance to go somewhere by himself and think. We talked of Enos and how he went out to a place where he could be alone. We will try to get him a cabin up in the mountains where he can at least spend one day. It was a thrill to me to be with him and talk as we did. He said that he often thinks of the talks that we have had. He says he has studied how Alma talked to his sons. He said that our talks together reminded him of that. I told him that he would be a better player when he returns. He said, "I'm not sure that I want to be." He said, "I believe that I will have the talent, but I'm not sure I will have the desire." He said, "It just doesn't seem to mean that much to me." We said many other things that I won't write now. Being with him lifts my spirits. He would be a wonderful missionary. I pray with all my heart that he will choose to go.

We then drove through the snow to Matt and Devin's apartment. Matt was not at home. Marinda and her friends were there. There was a wonderful article in the *Provo Herald* about Devin. It quoted him as saying that he felt so much had been done for him that he'd sure like to do something for others. We bade Devin good-bye and drove home to Salt Lake City. A truly wonderful day.

February 9, 1979. Since last week when I went to Provo and talked with Devin about his mission he has played two games. He didn't do well in either. He also had some rather poor practices, according to the coach. The coach asked him if something was bothering him. Devin said a mission was on his mind. He told the coach that he and I had talked about the possibility of his going this fall. He told the coach that he wanted him to know that so that he could try to recruit a forward for next year. The coach was somewhat alarmed by the news and concluded that my talk with Devin was the cause of Devin's lackluster play. The coach called me and asked to come and see Marilyn and me Wednesday night. We agreed and he came. We had a most cordial visit with him. He told me that he felt that my talk with Devin was ill timed. He felt it could cause Devin to play poorly and could result in the team not winning the conference championship. He also pled with us that Devin not go on a mission until he had played one more year. He said he just couldn't replace Devin next year. But he added that the year after he could. Marilyn felt that his request was reasonable. But I was not sure. It is my inward conviction after much thought and prayer that Devin should go this fall and not play another season. I told the coach that and he was obviously very disappointed. He departed cordially and that was it.

I prayed much that Devin would do well tonight and that the team would win. Then I'd know that I was not the cause of any heartbreak for the coach and for the team. But they didn't win and Devin didn't do well. He made one play that could have won the game but instead resulted in a foul on him and gave the other team the opportunity that they needed to win. The coach in the postgame show was very kind, but he did say, "Devin has a lot on his mind. I hope that he can shake it off and start to play like he has in the past."

And so my soul hurts. I realize that Devin is under some stress. But I also know that all athletes have slumps. I feel he is in a slump apart from his thoughts about his mission. I feel that he will come back. I know that God is the real coach. The game of life is far bigger than any game played under a roof by ten men. Life is filled with hard lessons. But they are lessons that teach much. God will not forsake us. Devin told me, "If we do good, things will turn out good." To me he is as one of the sons of Helaman. He always lifts my spirit.

It's eleven-thirty. The phone just rang. It was Devin. He said he was just checking to see how I am doing. He seemed in good spirits. He said he wanted to bring a girl to dinner Sunday. He asked me what I was doing. I told him I was writing in my journal the words which he had spoken, "If we do good, things will turn out good." After hearing that, he paused and then said, "I must not be doing good because in tonight's game things sure didn't turn out good. I sure didn't do good." I told him that tomorrow was another day. He told me I inspire him. But it is so much the other way around.

February 10, 1979. Tonight BYU won. Devin didn't do well and didn't even get in the second half. But the team won. Coach Arnold is handling things well. I felt responsible for Devin's present slump. But tonight they won so it makes it a bit easier. I believe that that will end the crisis and, as Coach Arnold said after the game, "Next week against Utah, Devin Durrant will be back and ready." I did all the dishes tonight while I listened to the game.

February 16, 1979. There is much excitement about the upcoming Utah game. People are sure hoping that Devin will do well. There are many rumors about why he has struggled lately, namely—"He is going to drop out of school"; "He has too many girls on his mind"; "He is going on a mission."

February 17, 1979. Devin and BYU beat Utah tonight by 25 points. Devin started slow, but then he became the star. It was such a thrill and such a relief to me. I have blamed myself for his poor play during the past games. But tonight he was his old self again. He is a winner. Devin has some good newspaper writeups about his game against Utah. I'd prayed so hard that he would come out of his slump and he did.

February 21, 1979. Met with a General Authority today. We had a long talk about when Devin should go on a mission. We discussed the coach's feelings. He also pointed out how hard it would be for Devin to go and return in the fall just before the season. He would have no time to get back in shape. He advised me that he felt it would be best for Devin to go on his mission in the spring a year hence. He felt that that way everyone, including the coach and the school, would feel good about it. After we talked, I felt good about such a decision and was anxious to talk it over with Devin.

February 23, 1979. Attended Devin's game. They beat Wyoming. Devin played well.

February 24, 1979. BYU had a hard game but finally won. Devin played a solid game. He plays smooth. Hard games sure are hard on me.

March 10, 1979. [The Y won the Conference Championship during Devin's freshman year. There were high expectations as the team went to Tucson, Arizona, to play San Francisco in the first game of the NCAA Tournament.]

At six-thirty in the morning VanWagoners came and picked up Marinda and me. At seven-thirty we departed in a six-passenger plane for Tucson, Arizona. Pilot: Henderson. Passengers: Brother and Sister VanWagoner, Richard Moyle and his son Mark, and Marinda and I. Three-hour flight on a clear, sunny day. Beautiful. Lake Powell and desert beautiful. Arrived one hour before game in a really festive mood. BYU against San Francisco. We lost bad. Devin did good but was bitterly disappointed. After the game when he came out of the locker room I hugged him. I told him, "You can never be as great as I am because you'll never have a son as great as you are." It was a sacred time with him. We walked outside and had a long talk. We flew home, arriving in Provo at seven-thirty in the evening. I was glad to be home.

March 20, 1979. Devin came to Salt Lake to see me at about nine o'clock. I called one of the General Authorities whom I knew well, and Devin and I went over to see him. He and Devin talked for about a half-hour. He told Devin that by going on a mission the next spring, all other things would fall into place. He told Devin many other things that inspired him. He then took us to lunch in the General Authority cafeteria. We met many of the Brethren there. I felt like the most blessed man in the world.

March 27, 1979. Received word this morning that Devin is going to China to play on a United States all-star team. Fred Roberts will also go. Coach Frank Arnold will go as an assistant coach. So Devin continues to have exciting things happen to him.

April 16, 1979. At six we went to the airport to pick up Devin. It was good to welcome him home from China. Later at home we sat down to a delicious roast beef dinner. Devin asked if he could give the prayer. He seemed choked up as he said, "We are grateful for this cold water, and for this delicious food, and for the blessings of living in the United States of America." It was very touching and seemed to reflect the profound influence the journey to China had on him.

September 18, 1979. Devin called tonight and told us that his ankle is broken. He will be in a cast for five weeks. That will take him to the time practice starts, and he'll then miss one week. He is fortunate that if it had to happen, it did when it did. He seems to take it in stride, or, I mean, on crutches.

September 26, 1979. Devin told me that Dick Motta, coach of the Washington Bullets, told someone, who then reported it to Devin, that he is a definite pro prospect as a guard. But Coach Motta added that a mission would veto all chances.

December 7, 1979. [On a team with Danny Ainge, Fred Roberts, Steve Trumbo, Alan Taylor, Scott Runia, Steve Craig, and Greg Kite, it looked like this season would be the greatest in history.]

In the evening we listened to Devin's basketball game in Tulsa, Oklahoma. He didn't do well—at least that is the way it sounded on radio. But with three seconds to go in the game and the score tied at 70 each, he got the ball, dribbled, and shot a long jump shot into the net. There was no time left and the Y had won. Devin was the hero of the game. It made me so happy that I could hardly contain myself. I had to go outside and walk and run and shout.

December 11, 1979. We went to Devin's game. He did well in the second half, making 10 of his 12 points then. It is fun to see him do well. But it sure is agonizing when he doesn't do well.

December 14, 1979. At seven we went to the Cougar Classic. Devin played an amazing game. He had 20 points in first half and ended with 25. The Y won easily.

December 15, 1979. Went shopping at the mall. Attended Devin's game. What a game! They won in three overtimes. Devin played like an all-American and made the all-tournament team. He made 24 points and played perfectly all night. The other coach said, "Whenever we had a chance to get ahead, Durrant would do his thing and we'd be in trouble again." Went to Coach Arnold's for a party.

December 22, 1979. Devin did well and BYU won a tight game in front of a very hostile Logan crowd. Devin felt a little disappointed because he missed some foul shots at the end of the game. He also made a bad pass. He made 12 points.

January 5, 1980. We arrived home just in time to see Devin play on TV. He did a great job—scoring 22 points and leading his team to a one-point victory. It was thrilling. It's nerve-racking but fun to have him playing.

January 12, 1980. Went to Provo to the BYU–Utah Basketball game. I was really nervous. I prayed long and fervently that Devin would have a great game, and he sure did. In the first half he was fantastic. He had 14 points and played flawlessly. I was proud.

BYU won by nearly 20 points, and Devin was judged the player of the game. We are grateful to the Lord for all of the blessings which he gives Devin.

January 26, 1980. BYU and Hawaii started a basketball game at ten-thirty our time. I was at a stake conference in Coalville. Marilyn and I spent the night at President Osmond's home. I listened. It was a tense game. I was in bed and because of the cold night and my nervousness during the game, I couldn't get my feet warm. Devin won the game with a foul pitch at five minutes past midnight: 34 to 33, BYU. Now I was too excited to sleep. I was fearful that sleep wouldn't come until I was in the morning session of stake conference.

January 29, 1980. Devin just called. He hopes he can get his mission call right after his last game so that he could leave around May first.

February 2, 1980. At one-thirty Devin and BYU began their televised game with New Mexico. The Y won handily. Devin made 13 points. He got four fouls on him right after the half and didn't get back in. I always want Devin to be the star. I suppose that that is the way it is for fathers.

February 12, 1980. Drove to Provo in the evening and watched a most exciting game with Utah State. Devin played really well. BYU won by one point. Devin had some rather sensational plays during this exciting encounter. The team is now ranked thirteenth in the nation. They have won nineteen games and lost 4. They could go a long way this year.

February 21, 1980. Tonight Devin had his greatest college game: 31 points, 7 assists, and 9 rebounds. He was spectacularly smooth. He was chosen the WAC's outstanding player for the second week in a row. BYU has now secured at least a tie for the conference championship.

February 23, 1980. We watched Devin and BYU defeat Wyoming; thus, the Y won the conference championship. After the game they interviewed Devin on Mountain West Television. They asked him if it was true that he was going on a mission. He spoke right up and told them the entire story. He was strong and most impressive. Among other things he said that he felt the Lord had given him so much that he desired to repay the Lord. I was thrilled beyond measure. The team came home at 10:32 P.M. We were at the airport to meet them.

February 28, 1980. In the evening we drove to Provo for Devin's game. He played a fantastic game—nine for nine from the field in the first half, 27 points all together. The Y won easily. I took Devin's missionary papers with me and he signed them in the Marriott Center. That seems quite fitting.

March 2, 1980. Devin's game was at one o'clock and was on TV. Devin did quite well. He made some nice shots: 14 points. As the game wound down, I had quite an empty feeling in my heart. We have seen him start and star in some thirty games at the Marriott Center in the past two years. Now, for a time and perhaps forever, it is over. We went to Coach Arnold's after for dinner with all of the parents and players.

March 8, 1980. Went to Ogden to see Devin's NCAA game. BYU was ahead at first and Devin was doing great. But then things changed. Clemson was too big. BYU lost by five. I was not as disappointed as I thought I would be. I wonder if I'm growing old or if my disappointment capacity is wearing out. At any rate I sensed that that loss was not one of the things worth worrying too much about. I was going to let Marilyn take the car home, and Devin would ride with her. I wanted to stay and watch another game and ride home with someone else. Just as the game was about to begin Devin came and said, "Come on, Pops." I replied, "I want to see this next game." He was firm and said, "No, Pops. You've got to come now. I need you." As we rode home we had much pleasant conversation. Finally at home, Devin requested a father's blessing. As I laid my hands on his head and prayed, I felt as if the Lord was in the room with us. Devin had asked me to bless him in his schoolwork, and in having patience answering all the questions that would be asked of him about his mission. He had also asked for help in preparing for his mission. I spoke to the Lord about all these things, and as I did I felt great power flow through me into him. I also felt prompted in regards to his future. When I said, "Amen," Devin arose and we embraced. We felt close to each other and to the Lord. We lost the big game but life is good.

March 9, 1980. I'm glad Devin's basketball career is over for at least two years. Two years? I wonder what will happen then. The future is uncertain but there is security in righteousness. I love the Lord.

March 12, 1980. I'm sure they assigned Devin to his mission today. He will know late this week or early next.

March 14, 1980. When I arrived home, Devin was there. He had received his mission call. I've never seen him so happy. He is going to Madrid, Spain. It's amazing but that seems like the perfect place for him. The Lord really sends people to just the right place. He is thrilled. It is fun to share the whole thing with him.

March 15, 1980. Arose and went with Marilyn to purchase some acrylic paints and brushes. The supplies cost me about $10.00. At nine-thirty in the morning I started painting a picture of Devin. I have a good photo of him playing basketball at the Marriott Center. I used that. Things really went well in the painting, better than I had ever dared to hope, because I haven't painted for a long time. Before I started I prayed to do well, and I believe because of my love for Devin and the help of the Lord that the painting is inspired. It really looks like him. I was impressed to try to put in a heavenly glow around him. I tried it and it worked. I think I will title the painting "Vision."

April 11, 1980. Devin came to see me at work. We ran into some of the Brethren. They were pleased to see him. They said, "It has just been approved that missionaries can play basketball on their preparation day." Devin said, "I've played enough of that for a while. All I want to do is learn Spanish and be a missionary."

April 25, 1980. Today we took Devin to the Missionary Training Center. On the way there we stopped at his former apartment. There I gave him a father's blessing. I was inspired by the Lord to make him many promises about his future in sports, but, more important, also in life. A half-hour later at the Missionary Training Center we went to a room with about thirty missionaries and their loved ones. After a short lecture on writing letters and not visiting and so on, it was time for Devin to go. We hugged our tall wonderful son and bade him good-bye. Tears filled my eyes. I will miss him so much. Even as I write this and glance up at the portrait which I painted of him and which hangs on our wall, my heart is filled with joy and also sorrow. I will not see him again for such a long time. But I'm deeply grateful that he is on his way to fight in such a glorious battle. So for now Devin is gone. He has much to learn and much to do. Time passes quickly and he will be home soon. All will be well with all of us—his family and him. God is good to us, and we love him. Last week Matt, Marilyn, Devin, and I went to the temple. Devin was deeply impressed. It gave him understanding. An older worker in the temple approached Devin and looked carefully at the name tag which had been pinned on Devin's shirt. Then, as he shook hands, he looked carefully at the name again and said, "Devin Durrant. Are you related to that Kevin Durrant, the BYU basketball player?" Devin smiled and said, "Well, sort of." His older brother, Matt, had to turn away to keep from revealing his restrained laughter. All through Devin's career our family has been greatly amused at the large number of people who called him Kevin. I shouldn't say we were all amused. It sort of irritated his mother.

May 9, 1980. I saw one of the Brethren today. He asked me about Devin and said, "Tell Devin that his mission will help his basketball ability and that he will be a far better player when he returns."

June 27, 1980. We arose early this morning and drove to the airport to bid farewell to Devin. After a visit of an hour or so, it was time for him to go. We walked down the long portal. Finally he said, "Let's say good-bye here, and I will go on alone." One by one he told everyone good-bye. He hugged his mother. He and I embraced. As I held him close, tears filled my eyes. I didn't want to let go, but he pulled away. Then he turned and with long enthusiastic strides headed away from us toward the final boarding. He didn't look back. As I watched him go, in my heart I could hear the enthusiastic refrains of "Rise and Shout" fade away, and the music of "I'll Go Where You Want Me to Go" filled my soul. We turned and with joyful sorrow made our way out of the airport. Marilyn said, "It will be a long two years without him." I advised her that at her age it would go quickly. She didn't acknowledge my comment.

1980–1982. [Devin filled a productive and inspiring mission in Spain. During those two years he never once shot a basketball at a hoop. What a joy it was to welcome him home.]

April 30, 1982. Margie, my dear secretary at the Genealogy Department where I work, placed a sign on my office door announcing the glorious fact that Devin was coming in on TWA at 8:37 tonight. I was so anxious that I couldn't work. I came home a little early and did a few things around the house. The entire family was excited to a fever pitch. At about seven we drove to the airport. We were soon at the gate where the plane would arrive. Grandma Burnham, Aunt Sharon and her family, and all of us were there. There just isn't anything as exciting as going to the airport to welcome home a missionary. It was a beautiful night. The plane came in right on time. As I saw it land I knew that Devin was on board and my heart pounded within me. I sort of stood back. After fifty or so people came into sight, I heard some gleeful shouts, and I knew Devin had appeared. In a second or two I saw him. I could not contain my emotions. My heart seemed to come up into my throat. What a thrill! He hugged his mother for a long time, and then he looked over and our eyes met. No words could describe what I felt. He came over and we embraced. I held him close. My Devin was home. As we drove home with him, we talked of many things. He looks healthy and happy. He has gained no weight. He has his hair almost crew cut short. He is home.

July 8, 1982. Devin continues to court Julie, who also served a mission. I think he loves her. He practices basketball each day either at the Y or the U of U. He is getting back into fine shape even though he says his game is far from what it was. One new player at the U of U watched Devin struggle to regain his strength and skills. He said to another, "So, this is the great Devin Durrant I've heard so much about. He's no good at all." I know by the way Devin works that someday that player will change his mind.

September 25, 1982. Sat by Devin and Julie at a football game. He seems real happy. He wouldn't say much to me about basketball, even though I made some inquiries. Finally he said, "Father, don't ask me the same questions everyone else asks me about basketball." He added, "You are my father. We've got more important things to talk about." I replied, "Oh, yeah. I almost forgot."

October 8, 1982. We went to the Marriott Center to watch Devin and his teammates play basketball. It was Media Day. Devin called me down where he was interviewed by KSL radio. He sure did well. The picture taking went on for an hour or so. Then they played. Devin was magnificent. He has great confidence. All the other players seem to respect him both as a man and as a player. He plays with greater intensity than he ever did before. I believe that while he was on his mission he did some things that make him a far greater player now. We had a nice visit with him after. He has many friends.

October 23, 1982. At 9:45 we all departed for Provo. Watched Devin practice basketball. To me he is picture perfect in the way he plays. But I'm his father. I like the way he gets a defensive rebound and starts down court all in one sweeping motion. He senses where everyone is.

November 25, 1982. Devin's game against sixth-ranked UCLA was on national cable TV. Devin played well. He made 21 points. His team lost by 3 points. He was very good at times. After the game he was ill.

November 29, 1982. Tonight's game was sad because the Cougars lost. Devin did well, scoring some 24 points, 20 in the second half. But his efforts were not enough. The team is suffering. We hope they can do better. We talked to him after the game. He had a black eye and seemed tired and discouraged.

December 3, 1982. Devin played on TV in Michigan. He was very hot and made ten for fourteen from the field. BYU lost.

December 10, 1982. BYU lost to Long Beach State. Devin has a severe cold and after the game he looked pretty tough. He has a bad cough.

December 11, 1982. We attended Devin's game. We were thrilled when the Cougars finally came up with a victory. They defeated Fordham. Devin sure was happy to win a game. We went to Coach Arnold's house after and had a party. The players, girlfriends, and families were all there. There was a happy feeling because of the victory.

December 14, 1982. Arrived at Logan just in time for the seven-thirty game with Utah State. Devin started well. The score was nearly even. But in the second half Utah State took a big lead. Devin had 24 points but wasn't dominant in the second half. The Y lost and Coach Arnold and all were very sad. Devin rode home with us. We had a good talk.

December 27, 1982. In the evening Marilyn, Mark, and I went to Sharon and Gene's. We had a delicious dinner and then watched BYU play St. John's at Madison Square Garden. The Y lost by ten points. Devin made 19 points and played well at times but also had problems at times.

December 28, 1982. We watched the last part of Devin's game on TV. The Y lost again. This time to St.

Joseph's. Devin made 27 points and was one of five men on the all-tournament team.

January 6, 1983. Went to Ogden tonight to watch Weber State play BYU. It was a very close game, and in two overtimes Weber finally won. Devin had a shot at the end of the first overtime that would have won it for BYU, but he missed by an inch or so. I was deeply disappointed at the outcome. The Y sure is having a difficult time getting some good breaks. They played better tonight. Devin rode home with us. Julie did also. He was sad but he maintains a cheerfulness that is quite a marvel. I gave him a kiss on the forehead as he went on his way.

February 3, 1983. Devin called tonight. He has been selected the Athlete of the Month for Utah. There will be a big article about it in the *Deseret News.* But they desire to wait until after the Utah game.

February 26, 1983. Devin and his Cougars won tonight. It was a great victory over UTEP at El Paso. Devin hit nine of ten shots and played well. It sure made us happy.

March 5, 1983. Devin looked good in warmups. The fans were the most enthusiastic I have ever seen. The game started and it was obvious that Utah was going to slow it down. It was a gruelling game. Devin did very well. The game ended in a tie. One, then two, then three overtimes. Finally the U won by two. It was a bitterly disappointing defeat. It will take a while to get over this one. Devin scored 25 points. After the game I couldn't sleep so I cleaned the kitchen. Devin came home at one o'clock, and he and I talked until two. He is disappointed but not discouraged. He doesn't feel that he is good enough to be a pro. He said he makes too many mistakes.

[The Y did not win the conference and were not invited to any postseason tournaments. Coach Arnold, who had done so much for Devin, was replaced as head coach. Devin married his sweetheart, Julie Mink.]

May 23, 1983. Devin came home from Colorado Springs. He did not make the Pan American team, but he was placed on the World Games team. He felt bad because during the tryouts he did well in the first two games, but in the third game he didn't do well. While there he had many interesting experiences with the other players and coaches. He met several pro scouts who seemed quite interested in him. One said he would play guard in the pros. He and Julie came to see me at work. They are happy. [They were wed several weeks earlier.]

June 29, 1983. Devin is in Missouri practicing for the World Games. He is doing well according to Julie. He scores about 11 points a game. He only gets to play less than half the game.

December 15, 1983. Devin is the leading scorer in the nation at this point. I hope that he will be able to keep it up. He and the team flew to Kentucky today to play in a tournament there. It is important that he does well there. I feel that he will.

December 16, 1983. Devin played early in the evening. He did well in the first half and quite well in the second. The team won and there was quite a thrill because now they get to play Kentucky. That was one of Devin's goals.

December 17, 1983. Devin played. It was on TV. To me, his father, he looked fantastic. He scored 22 points in the first half. The Y was ahead by two at the half against the number one team in the nation, Kentucky. Matt, who is now a student at Harvard, called and couldn't believe it. We turned on the radio, and he listened to much of the second half on the phone. Kentucky really poured it on in the second half and won a lop-sided victory. Devin was named the Most Valuable Player of the tournament. He scored 33 points in the game. Dreams seem to come true for him in Kentucky. The BYU publicity director is promoting him as a candidate for all-American, and this game will help.

December 23, 1983. Watched Devin play at five o'clock. He only made 19 points. He is now the leading scorer in the nation. This might drop him out of that rather pressure-packed title. The team won and we were happy. We took him to the hospital, where he had eleven stitches to bind up the cut over his eye. During the game blood had often streaked down his face. He looked like his hero, Rocky.

December 28, 1983. In the evening we watched Devin play on TV against UCLA. He had a great night and scored 36 points. The national commentators were impressed. He is having a fine year. The Y lost by 10 points but they played well.

January 14, 1984. Went down to BYU. Left at one o'clock. Got in a blizzard at the point of the mountain. Arrived after a two-hour drive. Devin and BYU played the U of U at three o'clock. Devin had 34 points, and the Y won in double overtime, 115 to 105. Devin played every minute of the game.

January 19, 1984. At ten-thirty we watched BYU play Hawaii on TV. The Y won, and Devin made 38 points. Went to bed at one o'clock in the morning very happy.

January 25, 1984. Devin continues to lead nation in scoring: 30.5 points per game.

February 2, 1984. The Y won and Devin did really well (against New Mexico). He made 27 points. He didn't score much at first, but as the game went on he got better.

February 11, 1984. Devin played at noon on national TV against Georgetown. He had his worst game of the season: 13 points. The Y lost by a long way. I sure did feel bad. I'm sure that Devin did also.

February 14, 1984. Went to Devin's game at the Y against Hawaii. He had a great game, particularly at the end. He hit his last eight shots, and he won the game with a last-second shot in the second overtime. To me he was an all-American tonight.

February 18, 1984. I watched BYU play Notre Dame. The Y won in a most thrilling game. Notre Dame defensed Devin perfectly and he only made 8 points, but he played well and was thrilled with a victory.

March 1, 1984. Went to BYU in the evening. Devin scored 35 points and played brilliantly as the Y rolled over UTEP. They were ranked eighth in the nation but the Y handled them easily. It sure is good to win. It was on regional TV and will help Devin's success.

March 3, 1984. Devin played his final game in the Marriott Center. I gave the opening prayer. He played brilliantly. He scored 34 points and the team won. He was honored after the game by the 23,000 fans. When he received a block Y blanket, all stood and applauded him. He then turned to the north and applauded the fans, then did the same to those on the west, and so on in all four directions. He is much loved. I had deep emotions as it all ended. We had made our last journey to the Marriott Center to see our son, the great Devin Durrant, play basketball. He set a new single-season BYU scoring record, and they gave him the game ball. I'm sort of glad it is over. He has no regrets nor do I. He started every game during his four-year career. He and his teammates won three WAC championships. He was named to three all-American teams. The Lord has truly blessed him, and we rejoice with him at his success.

March 15, 1984. Devin and BYU played tonight in the NCAA Tournament. I was deeply thrilled as the Y won over a very good team from the University of Alabama at Birmingham. They were playing on their home court, but BYU played exceptionally well and won 84 to 68. Devin had a great game. Saturday we play Kentucky. They are very good. So we will likely lose. But with tonight's victory we have won 20 games. So that makes a very successful season. I'm sure Devin is happy. He deserves that. He has worked hard and made many sacrifices.

March 17, 1984. We watched BYU play Kentucky. It was a disaster. Kentucky is just too good. Devin did well and made 28 points, but the Cougars just weren't in it. So Devin has completed his college career.

I'm glad. I'm sad. I'm sorry. I'm happy. It is good it is over. I will miss the pregame excitement. I'll miss the exhilarating pride that came when he did well, which was so very often. Even as I write I feel emotion rise up in my soul. His career has been like a mighty miracle. He seemed to develop line upon line and talent upon talent. The Lord has truly blessed him. He loves the Lord. Many look to him as an example. I thank God for his generous treatment of Devin.

Epilogue

April 7, 1984. At four-thirty Devin and I drove to the University Hospital, where we visited a fourteen-year-old boy who has leukemia. The boy loves Devin, and the family felt it would be a great blessing if Devin could visit him. The boy was desperately ill but was pleased to see Devin. We then drove to the Tabernacle. There we were met by Warren, Mark, Dwight, and Paul. We went to door number six, where Darson Roper let us all in. We were seated on the front row. Devin was seated to the right of the Brethren—on the stand. Elder Hinkley conducted. He announced the opening song and prayer. Then he said, "The choir will now sing, after which our first speaker will be that great basketball champ from BYU, Devin Durrant." He added, "Devin is as much a star at the pulpit as he is on the basketball court." The people were audibly pleased. (I understand that they cheered at the TV broadcast at the Marriott Center.) During the last verse of the opening song, Devin took the long walk to the pulpit. He arrived a little early and sat on the edge of Elder Faust's chair. Then the time came. He stood and began to speak, and oh, how he did speak! I don't think any father has ever been so proud. It was a magnificent talk. Tears filled my eyes as he spoke of seeking reasons to go on a mission rather than reasons not to go. He also spoke of the joys that all worthy young men can find in missionary service, and closed by sharing his testimony of Jesus Christ and his Church. It was an evening I shall never forget.

A dad, a boy, a ball, and a call. Add all that up and the result is a multitude of blessings cemented together with much love.

All the best to all you sports fans, or, I should say, all you champs!